Modern Nature-Inspired Quilts

Make 25 Beautiful Projects — No Rulers or Templates Required

BERNADETTE MAYR

In cooperation with Irmgard Stängl

Photographs by Sabine Münch

FOX CHAPEL
PUBLISHING

Foreword

This book takes Modern Quilting to a whole new level. I love quick-piecing techniques and innovative concepts, and, having designed many books about simplified quilting techniques and tricks, I am always on the lookout for a valuable addition to my library. Now, with this innovative book by Bernadette Mayr, I am inspired to learn a whole new set of skills.

When I first saw this book, it was in the original German. I was amazed and wanted to immediately start using the fabulous free-cut techniques and make some of the beautiful quilts. I didn't even need to be able to read the words to understand just how great the information in this book is. And now here it is, translated into English, so anyone can get started.

The nature-inspired designs are riveting, the skills are invaluable, and the book as a whole is truly a piece of art. It is a pleasure and a privilege to have this book available in English. I hope you enjoy practicing these techniques and creating these beautiful projects. Enjoy!

—Suzanne McNeill

Original edition © 2013
World rights reserved by Christophorus Verlag GmbH & Co. KG, Freiburg, Germany
Original German title: Mayr, Bernadette: Landschaftsimpressionen. Patchworkmotive in freier Schneidetechnik.

Credits for the German Edition
Design and quilt making: Bernadette Mayr; proofreading: Claudia Schmidt; editor: Angelika Klein; photography: Sabine Münch; styling: Gundula Manson; technical drawings: Bernadette Mayr

ISBN 978-1-57421-860-2

Modern Nature-Inspired Quilts is an unabridged translation of the original German book. This version published by New Design Originals Corporation, an imprint of Fox Chapel Publishing Company, Inc., East Petersburg, PA.

Library of Congress Cataloging-in-Publication Data
Mayr, Bernadette, 1952-
  [Landschafts-Impressionen. English]
  Modern nature-inspired quilts / Bernadette Mayr.
    pages cm
  Translation of: Landschafts-Impressionen.
  Includes index.
  ISBN 978-1-57421-860-2
  1. Quilting--Patterns. 2. Quilts. 3. Nature in art. I. Title.
  TT835.M389513 2014
  746.46--dc23
                    2014004204

Printed in China
First printing

Introduction

My sister and I have had great fun making the quilts for this book. Of course, we had a few setbacks and there were some difficulties to overcome, but we have come to the conclusion that they can be divided into just two categories: human error and "acts of God."

For example, it's human error when you cut out something incorrectly, or sew in a piece of fabric with the reverse side showing, or get a block the wrong way round, even though it was laid out correctly, and only notice when everything has been sewn together. Or when making a quilt of hexagons, you suddenly feel the paper templates you've forgotten to remove before adding the backing. It's a particularly impressive human error when you prewash a piece of fabric that has been printed for hand quilting. It's very annoying and is usually because you've not been paying attention. Human error is human error, but it's a different matter when it comes to "acts of God."

In quilting terms, we don't mean "acts of God" on a biblical scale—like being plunged into sudden darkness after a bolt of lightning—but rather on a smaller scale, like when the bobbin thread runs out. It particularly likes to run out just when you've pinned out a complicated row to fit exactly seam to seam and begin to sew carefully from top to bottom; by the time you realize that you've been working without thread, all the pins have already been removed. And all that's required to ruin a rotary cutter is for a single pin to get in the way of the blade—one that wasn't

there a second ago. Acts of God are also at work when you run out of fabric and you can't get any more; you end up rummaging around in the trash for scraps, or—if you can't find anything there—having to change the design of the entire quilt. Necessity is the mother of invention. How often do you have to go searching for a piece of fabric, ruler, quilting needle, or rotary cutter? The seam ripper in particular! Do sewing rooms have gremlins? I really think they might.

If all this seems rather familiar, then you'll know that, equally, miracles can happen too—the times when there's just enough thread down to the last half an inch, when every piece of fabric has been correctly cut, and a complicated border piece fits, even though you didn't do any working out beforehand.

Ask any patchworker what problems they had to overcome when making this or that quilt and you'll soon find out that you are not alone.

Enjoy your sewing!

—Bernadette Mayr

Yes, luckily there are two of us. We make silly mistakes and there's never a dull moment. Perhaps the day will come when we have finally seen everything.

—Irmgard Stängl

Irmgard Stängl and Bernadette Mayr

Bernadette Mayr is one of the most famous quilt artists in Germany. She has published a half-dozen successful books about quilting and the free form cutting technique, her area of specialty, and has won many awards over the years for her work, including Best of Country for her quilt "Manhattan" at the World Quilt Competition in 2007. She also translates and proofreads textile trade books and is an accomplished painter and drawer. She is currently featured at quilt exhibitions and holds frequent quilting, drawing, and painting workshops around Germany. Visit her at her website: www.Bernadette-Mayr.de.

Acknowledgments

I would like to thank my sister Irmgard for sharing the work and for her support in making so many quilts, my friend Gundula for the "comprehension test" and for proofreading, Claudia Pfeil for her delightful tutorials in long-arm quilting, and Sabine Münch from Berlin for the wonderful photographs.

Contents

CUTTING SHAPES

STRIPS

Materials

Equipment

You'll need a normal household sewing machine, a cutting mat (at least 18" x 24" [45 x 60cm] in size), a rotary cutter (1¾" [45mm] diameter) and the usual sewing notions, such as needles, thread, pins, scissors, chalk wheel, etc. A pin board for designs will also be useful or a large cloth on which you can pin out your fabric pieces. A steam iron is also recommended for pressing, or you can use a spray bottle (the type you'd use to water plants) to dampen the fabrics before pressing.

Rulers

You will need a ruler to cut blocks of equal size, to create even stripes, to make edging strips, to help when cutting lots of strips and fabric pieces of the same size, and to straighten outside edges. Keep a long 6" x 24" (15 x 60cm) quilting ruler handy, as well as an 8" (20cm) square ruler. 4" (10cm)-wide quilting rulers also come in very handy.

Fabrics

Use good-quality cotton fabrics that are easy to cut and press, such as craft fabrics. Make sure you have a good variety of fabrics in a color group. You can use plain fabrics, prints, and hand-dyed or batik fabric. You should also have some interesting black-and-white striped fabrics in your sewing basket.

Lengths of fabric

If you are buying fabric without a particular project in mind, I recommend buying a "regular quarter" (9" [25cm] strip of fabric cut from selvage to selvage from the bolt) in each color. A "fat quarter" (approx. 18" x 22" [50 x 55cm]) is made by cutting an 18" x 44" (50 x 110cm) piece of fabric in half down the center fold.

Exact lengths are given in the quilting projects in case you need to go to the stores specially to buy fabric: the fabric lengths are based on craft fabrics approx. 44" (110cm) wide. Bear in mind that you will often need more fabric if you are using freehand rather than traditional patchwork

techniques, as excess fabric at the seams always needs to be trimmed back, pieces that are too large have to be cut to size, and any gaps have to be filled with fabric. Many of the projects will tell you how many sections can be cut and/or sewn from each strip of fabric, so it is possible to calculate in advance how much fabric is required for other quilt sizes or your own variations.

Batting

All the quilts, wall hangings, and pillows described are filled with medium-thickness polyester batting. You can use any other batting that you are familiar with: cotton or wool batting is flatter and heavier than polyester batting, but is preferred by many quilters due to its natural fibers.

Threads

You can join colored fabrics with threads in neutral shades such as gray, beige, or brown. Only use black or white thread for black or white quilts. Quilting threads should match the color of the fabric, just as the thread color for appliqué should match the color of the appliqué motifs that will appear on the top layer when the quilt is finished.

Techniques

Cutting freehand

Freehand cutting involves working without a ruler or a template. Lay the fabric out in front of you on the cutting mat and cut it with the rotary cutter. Line up the fabric using the gridlines of your cutting mat and rely on judging it by eye. Use the first piece you cut as a guide and a shape to copy. It's normal for the fabric pieces and the seams to shift slightly when being joined up. Trim off any excess fabric, or make up smaller pieces to the correct size by sewing them together.

You will soon be able to judge accurately how much fabric will be needed for the seam allowances. When cutting a number of strips or squares, lay the ruler along the length you want, but be generous; you don't need to measure exactly as it doesn't need to be correct to the last fraction of an inch.

Most projects include a step to trim all the blocks to the same size, and this is where you should use a ruler and measure exactly.

Pressing

When cutting and sewing fabrics freehand, you don't have to be concerned about pulling, stretching, or wetting the fabric, or being too free with the steam iron, and you don't have to worry about pulling a block out of shape either; it's going to be cut to size anyway.

Use a steam iron, or dampen fabrics with a spray bottle like the type you'd use to water plants. Press the dampened fabrics from the wrong side first in order to flatten the seam allowances, then turn the fabric and press again on the right side to press the seams. Pull the edges of the fabric away from the iron a little to avoid creases. Press all the seam allowances to one side rather than pressing them flat. Press the seam allowances of narrow, inset strips to the background side, even if the background fabric is light-colored—there will not be enough space for both seam allowances within the strip. Always press from the wrong side first and then press again from the right side of the fabric.

For curved seams, press the seam allowances to the side on which the seams themselves naturally lie; this will be determined by the thickness of the fabric and the seams that were sewn first. If you are joining blocks to make the front panel of a quilt, follow the rules for arranging seam allowances specified in Lesson 10: Assembling Blocks of Equal Size. Dampen these seams as well when you're pressing from the wrong side, placing the iron so that the seam allowances lie in the right direction; you can then press again from the right side. Press the seam allowances of edging strips to lie to the outside; only the seam allowances of Y-shaped seams (e.g. in diagonal corners) are pressed out.

Working from a sewing plan

A sewing plan is provided for many of the quilts to give an overview of the position of individual pieces of fabric; it should make things easier when joining these together. Think of the sewing plan as just a suggestion; if you come up with a different arrangement as you work, follow that instead, but always remember that freehand cutting and your personal style of working may mean that dimensions and positioning can change at any time. Bear this in mind as you work but don't let it worry you too much!

Quilting

The quilts in this book were quilted freehand using a long arm sewing machine. The suggested quilting patterns will often also work if you are quilting by hand or using a normal household sewing machine. You can choose for yourself which approach you prefer.

Tip
Quilt busy quilts with simple patterns, quilt plain quilts with a lively pattern.

CUTTING SHAPES

Lesson 1:
Strips, Squares, Triangles
Projects: Lightning strikes, Snowbreaks, Tulip fields, Grand Prismatic Spring, Spruce plantation, Limestone landscape, Desert roses, Four seasons: Tree in spring, Tree in summer, Tree in the fall, Tree in winter.

Strips
Lay the folded fabric flat on your cutting mat with as much of the fabric on the table as possible. Align one of the folded edges of the fabric with one of the grid lines on the cutting mat and ensure the cutting lines are at right angles with the fabric. Cut the fabric from selvage to selvage, making the strips as wide as required for your planned pieces. You can cut several layers of fabric at the same time. Hold the fabric securely on the cutting mat with your fingertips, but be careful with the rotary cutter; you could injure yourself as there is no ruler edge to offer protection. Cut through the fabric as swiftly as possible, judging it by eye; it doesn't have to be exact to the last fraction of an inch and it won't matter if your cutting line isn't exactly straight.

Squares/rectangles
Lay one to four strips of fabric on top of one another on the cutting mat. Cut off the selvage if there is any. Align the right- or left-hand edge (depending on whether you're right- or left-handed) with one of the grid lines. Work to the nearest grid line for the size desired for your pieces of fabric.

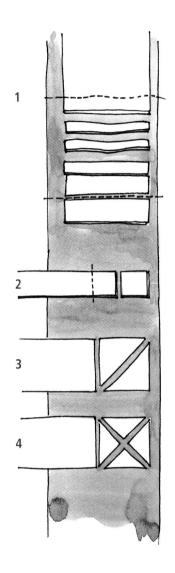

1

2

3

4

Place the rotary cutter at the lower edge of the fabric and cut through all the layers of fabric at once, toward the top, without using a ruler. It won't matter if your cutting line isn't exactly straight.

Triangles
Cut the strips of fabric into squares of the appropriate size and divide them diagonally into 2 triangles, or cut larger squares along both diagonals to make 4 triangles. There is no need to use a ruler when cutting.

1: Lay the folded fabric on the cutting mat. Cut strips to desired length, using the grid lines of the cutting mat as a guide. Cut the strips either freehand or with a ruler, but there's no need to measure to the last fraction of an inch.

2: Cut squares and/or rectangles from the strips to the desired size. Push the rotary cutter vertically from the bottom to the top of the fabric, using the grid lines of the cutting mat as a guide.

3: Cut a square of fabric in half diagonally to make 2 triangles; the straight grain will run along the short sides.

4: Cut a square of fabric along both diagonals to make 4 triangles; the straight grain will run along the long sides.

Tip
Use a ruler if you have a large number of squares, rectangles, or triangles to cut for a large quilt. This will prevent you from unintentionally cutting the shapes a little bit smaller or larger at every cut and thus unnecessarily wasting material. Just use the ruler as a straight edge for the rotary cutter, you don't need to make exact measurements.

Lesson 2:
Two-piece Blocks
Projects: Lightning strikes, Snowbreaks, Tulip fields, Grand Prismatic Spring

Cutting out rectangles and dividing them
Cut out some rectangles in the colors and sizes indicated in the project instructions.

Place one rectangle on top of another of a different color. Both fabrics should lie lengthways with the right side uppermost. Cut the 2 rectangles in half down the middle.

Be sure to cut at a slight angle and do NOT follow the grid lines of the cutting mat.

Don't make the cut for the next pair of fabrics identical; angle the cutter slightly differently.

Swapping colors
Arrange the left-hand piece of the upper fabric with the right-hand piece of the lower fabric and vice versa.

Joining two-piece blocks
Join the seam between the 2 halves. Open out the block and press the seam allowances to the darker fabric side. Cut all the blocks to an exact square, taking the dimensions from the project instructions.

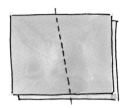

Place 2 rectangles on top of one another, right sides up and lengthways on the cutting mat. Cut them in half at a slight angle.

Swap over the colors: place the top left-hand piece and the bottom right-hand piece together and vice versa. Join both pieces and trim to make a square block.

Lesson 3:
Four-piece Blocks
Projects: Strawberry fields, Quarry face, Flower carpet

Cutting squares
Cut some rectangles in the colors and sizes indicated in the project instructions.

Place 4 squares in the indicated colors one on top of the other, all right sides up. Place the pieces on the cutting mat and cut into quarters, from top to bottom and from side to side.

Be sure to cut at a slight angle and do NOT follow the grid lines of the cutting mat. Don't make the cuts for the next pile of fabrics identical; angle the cutter slightly differently.

Sorting four-piece blocks
Number each pile in your head from left to right, starting top left.

Take pile 1 and lay out the 4 pieces of fabric (without rotating them) in position 1 of the four-piece blocks. Now lay out the 4 pieces from pile 2 in position 2 (starting at the second square, so the colors are mixed). Place the pieces from pile 3 in position 3, starting at the third square, and place the pieces from pile 4 in position 4, starting at the fourth square. Each group of 4 should now be composed of 4 different fabrics.

Tip
Try to avoid rotating the pieces. If this does happen, sort all the pieces of fabric back and start again from the beginning.

Lesson 2

Joining four-piece blocks

Place the 2 right-hand pieces of fabric on top of the left-hand ones, right sides facing. Sew along the right-hand edge, following the edge of the material using the foot of the sewing machine as a rough guide. Make sure you start with the upper pieces of fabric. Let the corners of the seam allowances overhang a little at the center—this is not important for the pattern but it will make sewing easier. The edges of the blocks will always be a little irregular using this technique, especially when the cuts are made at a sharp angle.

The seams don't have to meet exactly in the center.

Place the next pair of fabric pieces under the foot of the the sewing machine without cutting the thread linking it to the first pair.

Open out both pairs of fabric pieces and arrange them to make the horizontal seam, right sides facing; if you don't cut the thread, you can't get the pieces in the wrong position.

Now place both pairs of pieces together lengthways with the connecting threads on the right. Sew along the right-hand edge and press the seam allowances in opposite directions.

Open out the finished four-piece block. Press it first from the wrong side to flatten the seam allowances and then press from the right side. Trim the block to an exact square, following the dimensions given in the project instructions.

Cutting: make piles of 4 squares and cut into quarters at a slight angle horizontally and vertically. Number the piles in your head (from left to right).

Sorting: place a piece from pile 1 in each position 1, a piece from pile 2 in each position 2 (start at the second square so the colors are mixed), and so on. There should be one piece of each fabric in each of the blocks.

Joining up: place the right-hand pieces on top of the left-hand ones. Overhang the seam allowances slightly at the center. Join up in pairs along the right-hand edge; don't cut the thread.

Open up the pairs of fabric pieces, place them together and sew up the horizontal seam. Press the seam allowances in opposite directions.

Open up the block and press, then trim to form an exact square.

Lesson 4:
Narrow Triangles

Projects: Spruce plantation,
Limestone landscape

For the color, size, and number of pieces of fabric, refer to the instructions for the project in question.

Dividing rectangles

Place 2 rectangles of fabric of different colors on top of one another; the rectangles should lie lengthways on the cutting mat with right sides up. Place the rotary cutter at the lower edge, approx. ½"–1¼" (1–3cm) (depending on the project) in from the bottom right-hand corner and cut diagonally upward to roughly the center of the top edge. Push the pieces of fabric apart a little. Starting from the opposite bottom edge, a little in from the bottom left-hand corner, cut toward the top to meet the first cutting line. The top point of the triangle should be approx. 1¼"–1½" (3–4cm) below the top edge of the rectangle. Swap over the colors and sew up.

> **Tip**
> It doesn't matter if you start cutting on the right or left side (left-handers might like to start on the left). Either way, the first cut is always longer and the second shorter.

Joining the triangles

Start with the short seam (see arrow), sewing from the bottom edge of the fabric. Place the triangle on top of the left-hand background piece, right sides facing, allowing the seam allowance at the tip of the triangle to overhang a little. Join the pieces and open out the workpiece. Press the seam allowance toward the triangle. Trim the excess seam allowance at the top, following the line of the triangle edge. Join the right-hand background piece to the longer seam, letting the corner of the seam allowance of the triangle overhang at the tip again. Trim the block to the correct size; the dimensions are given in the projects, but slight alterations may be needed depending on your seam allowance or sewing technique.

Place 2 rectangles of different colored fabric on top of one another, right sides up.

Make the first cut from the bottom edge, starting a little way in from the corner, up to the top edge. Move the pieces apart a little.

The second cut is made from the bottom edge, again a little in from the corner, up to join the first cut.

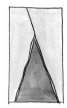 

Swap over the colors.

Sewing: join the short seam first, starting from the bottom. Press the seam allowances toward the triangle.

Trim the seam allowance in line with edge of the triangle.

Join the long seam. Press the block and trim to the correct size.

Lightning Strikes
Pillow, 20" x 20" (50 x 50cm)

The traditional version of this pattern is called "fence rail" and is one of the easiest patchwork patterns to make. It feels good when you start working without a ruler and are cutting through two layers of fabric at a time. Our "lightning strikes" adaptation is also easy as pie—all you are really doing is joining up squares.

▓ Materials
Fabrics for 1 pillow
- 16" (40cm) white
- 16" (40cm) black

Other materials
- 24" x 24" (60 x 60cm) white backing fabric (for the pillowcase front)
- 24" x 24" (60 x 60cm) batting
- 24" x 24" (60 x 60cm) white backing fabric (for the back of the pillowcase, with button fastening)
- 16" (40cm) white zipper, if required
- quilting thread in white

Cutting guide
4" (10cm) fabric, cut from selvage to selvage, is enough to make eight 4" x 4¾" (10 x 12cm) rectangles.

▓ Method
49 two-piece blocks
(Lesson 1: Strips, squares, triangles, and Lesson 2: Two-piece blocks)
Cut 25 rectangles approx. 4" x 4¾" (10 x 12cm) from both the black and the white fabrics (be generous when cutting). Place a white and a black rectangle together lengthways on the cutting mat, both right sides up. Make a diagonal cut roughly down the center of both fabrics. Alter the cutting angle for each pair to

make the two-piece blocks as irregular as possible. Swap over the colors of each pair. Join up the 2 halves of fabric. Press and trim each block to an exact square; ours were 3½" x 3½" (9 x 9cm).

Sewing plan
Place the blocks in 7 rows of 7 squares each.
1st row: black right, black top, black right, black top, and so on.
2nd row: black top, black right, black top, black on the right, and so on.
3rd row: as 1st row.
4th row: as 2nd row, and so on. The black and white fabrics will form diagonal zigzag lines across the pillow.

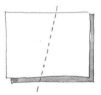

Place a white and a black rectangle (4" x 4¾" [10 x 12cm]) of fabric together, both right sides up. Cut at an angle, varying the angle slightly for each successive pair of rectangles.

Swap over the colors and join the halves. Press and cut to an exact square (4" x 4" [9 x 9cm]).

Assembly
(Lesson 10)
Assemble the pillowcase pieces following the instructions for assembling blocks of equal size.

Making up the quilt and quilting
(Lessons 12 and 13)
Place the pillow backing fabric, batting, and pressed front panel on top of one another. Using the sewing machine, quilt a pattern onto the white fabric that will easily accommodate the corners; I went for an agave leaf pattern. Quilt by hand using white thread at a spacing of approx. ½" (1cm) from the black seams.

Finishing
(Lesson 15)
Sew up the pillowcase and fill with a pillow form.

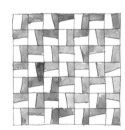

Fence rail pattern—lightning strikes!

Quilting suggestion.

Snowbreaks
94½" x 90½" (240 x 230cm)

Snowbreaks are an everyday sight in the Allgäu in Germany during the winter and keep the roads clear of snowdrifts. The older type are made of wood but the newer models are orange or made of green plastic netting, which would provide great inspiration for a quilt design.

■ Materials
Fabrics

- 7¾ yd. (7m) pure white (or a corresponding length of bedsheet fabric) for the snowdrifts and the border
- 2¼ yd. (2m) in total of one kind or a variety of different blue-and-white striped fabrics (stripe width ⅛"–³⁄₁₆"[3–5 mm]) for the fences
- 24" (60cm) blue-and-white striped fabric for the binding

Other materials

- 103" x 99" (260 x 250cm) backing fabric
- 103" x 99" (260 x 250cm) batting
- quilting thread in white

Cutting guide

6" (15cm) of fabric, cut from selvage to selvage, is enough to make eight 6" x 5" (15 x 13cm) rectangles. 4¾" (12cm) of fabric, cut from selvage to selvage, is enough to make nine 4¾" (12cm) squares.

■ Method
Preparation

Cut nine 2¾" (7cm)-wide white strips and set aside for the border. Cut ten 2½" (6cm)-wide strips from one of the striped fabrics and set aside for the binding.

190 two-piece blocks

(Lesson 1: Strips, squares, triangles and Lesson 2: Two-piece blocks)
Cut ninety-five 6" x 5" (15 x 13cm) rectangles from the white fabric and 95 of the same from the striped fabrics. For the striped fabrics, first cut 6" (15cm)-wide strips from selvage to selvage and then divide these into 5" (13cm)-wide rectangles. This will ensure the stripes run along the long side of the rectangles. Place a white rectangle and a striped rectangle together lengthways on the cutting mat, both right sides up. Cut down the center of both fabrics at an angle. Swap over the colors. Join up the 2 different colored pieces of fabric. Vary the cutting angle slightly to make the two-piece blocks as irregular as possible. Press and cut all the blocks to an exact square: ours were 4¾" x 4¾" (12 x 12cm). Keep blocks with the same striped fabric together, so you can link them up later when you assemble the pieces for the quilt.

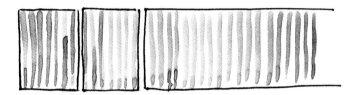

Cutting the rectangles: the stripes should run along the long edge.

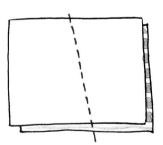

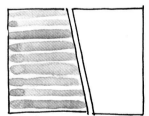

Place 2 rectangles (6" x 5" [15 x 13cm]) of fabric together, both right sides up. Cut in half at a slight angle. Vary the cutting angle with each pair of rectangles.

Rearrange the colors and join. Trim to an exact square (4¾" x 4¾" [12 x 12cm]).

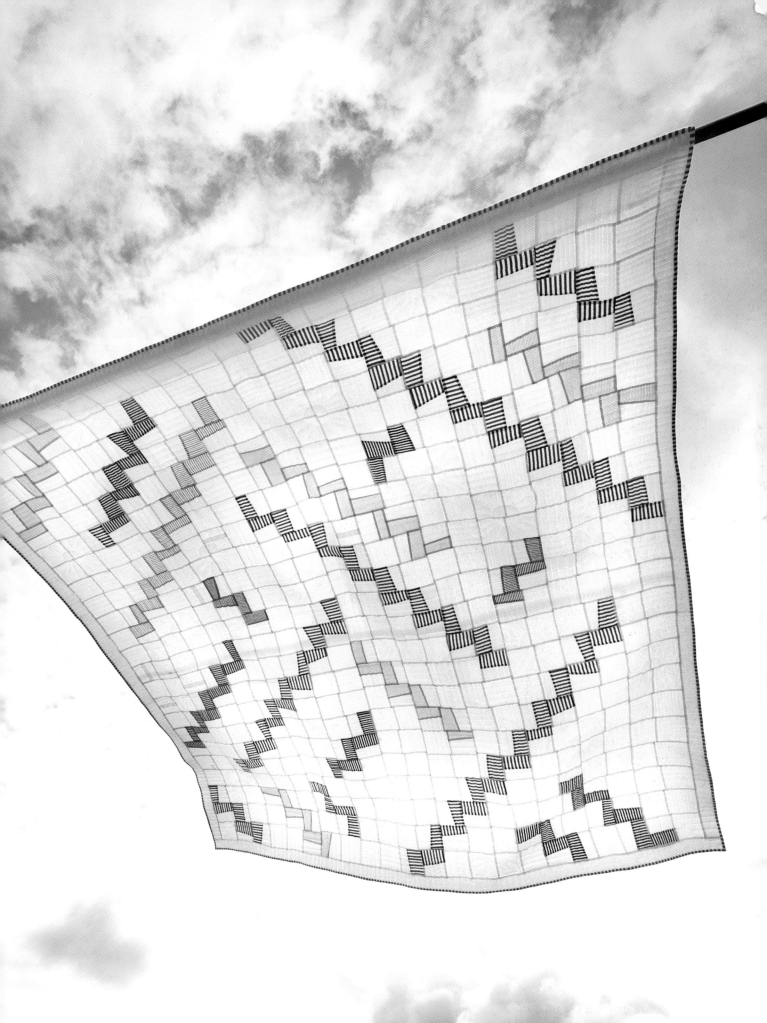

316 white squares

For the snowdrifts you will need 316 squares the same size as the two-piece blocks; ours were exactly 4¾" x 4¾" (12 x 12cm).

Sewing plan

Find a surface big enough to lay out the entire quilt. Lay out 23 horizontal rows of 22 blocks each, following the sewing plan, or make up your own arrangement. Lay out your snow fences with matching striped fabrics so they form diagonal rows.

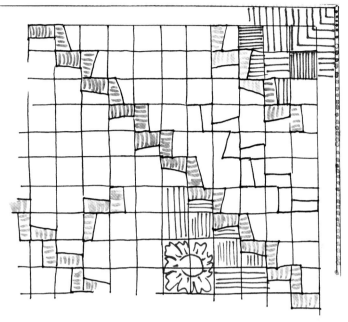

Sewing plan, border design, and quilting suggestion.

Key to the table abbreviations: W = white square; Br/Bl/Bt/Bb = two-piece block with the striped part to the right, to the left, at the top, or at the bottom.

From the top:

Row 1: 3W Br 7W Bt Bl 5W Bl 3W
Row 2: 2W Br Bt 2W Br 5W Bt Bl 4W Bt Bl 2W
Row 3: 1W Br Bt 2W Br Bt 1W Br 4W Bt Bl 4W Bt Bl 1W
Row 4: Br Bt 2W Br Bt 1W Br Bt 5W Bt Bl 1W Br Bb 1W Bt Bl
Row 5: Bt 2W Br Bt 1W Br Bt 1W Bb 5W Bt Bl 1W Br Bb 2W
Row 6: 2W Br Bt 1W Br Bt 2W Br Bb 2W Bb Bl 1W Bt Bl 1W Br Bb 1W
Row 7: 4W Br Bt 2W Bl 1W Br Bb 1W Bl 3W Bt Bl 1W Br Bb (not Bt!)
Row 8: 3W Br Bt 3W Bt Bl 1W Br Bb 5W Bt Bl 2W
Row 9: 2W Br Bt 5W Bt Bl 1W Br Bb 5W Bt Bl 1W
Row 10: 1W Br Bt 2W Bl 4W Bt Bl 1W Br Bb 5W Bt Bl
Row 11: 1W Bt 3W Bt Bl 4W Bt Bl 4W Br 3W Bt
Row 12: 6W Bt 2W Br 2W Bt Bl 2W Br Bt 4W
Row 13: 4W Br 3W Br Bt 3W Bt Bl 1W Bt 5W
Row 14: 3W Br Bt 2W Br Bt 1W Bl 3W Bt Bl 3W Br 2W
Row 15: 2W Br Bt 2W Br Bt 2W Bt Bl 3W Bt 2W Br Bt 2W
Row 16: 1W Br Bt 2W Br Bt 4W Bt Bl 4W Br Bt 3W
Row 17: Br Bt 2W Br Bt 3W Br 2W Bt Bl 2W Br Bt 4W
Row 18: Bt 2W Br Bt 3W Br Bt 3W Bt 1W Br Bt 5W
Row 19: 2W Br Bt 3W Br Bt 5W Br Bt 6W
Row 20: 6W Bb 6W Br Bt 2W Bb 4W
Row 21: Bl 2W Bt Bl 1W Br Bb 4W Br Bt 3W Br Bb 3W
Row 22: Bt Bl 2W Bt Bl 1W Br 3W Br Bt 2W Bt Bl 1W Br Bb 2W
Row 23: 1W Bt Bl 2W Bt Bl 3W Br Bt 4W Bt Bl 1W Br Bb 1W

Assembly
(Lesson 10)

Join up the front of the quilt, following the instructions for assembling blocks of equal size.

Adding the border
(Lesson 11)

Sew a 2¾" (7cm)-wide strip around all the edges.

Making up the quilt and quilting
(Lessons 12 and 13)

Place the backing, batting, and pressed front panel on top of one another. Quilt a striped pattern horizontally and vertically at intervals of approx. ⅜"–¾" (1–2cm) across one, two, or three squares. The stripes that continue right to the edge should always be vertical to the edge of the quilt. Quilt some snow flowers across the quilt, making sure they are always centered in a group of 4 white squares.

Binding
(Lesson 14)

Bind the quilt with folded strips of straight-cut, blue-and-white striped fabric, cut to a width of 2½" (6cm).

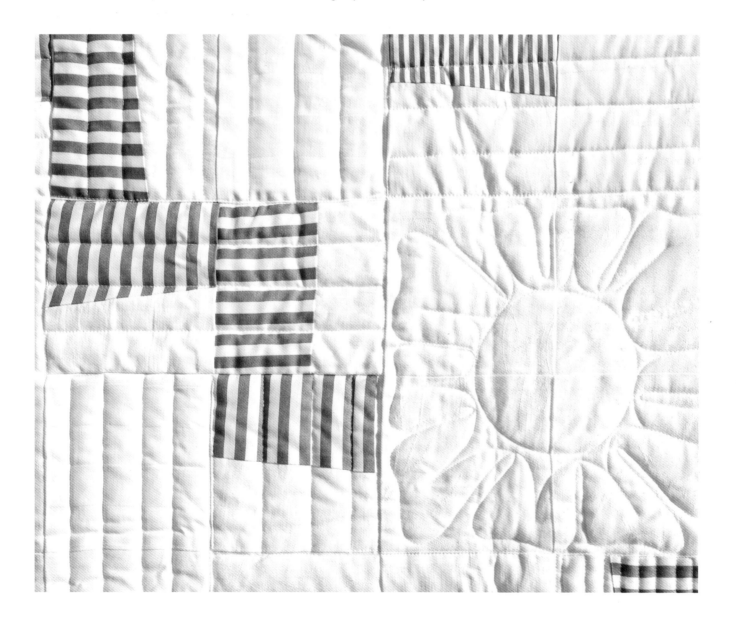

Tulip Fields
80¾" x 65" (205 x 165cm)

What could be more Dutch than tulip fields and windmills? They provide the inspiration for this design. The vivid green of the grass sets off the bold colors of the flowers. This quilt is striking and easy to sew.

■ Materials
Fabrics

- 8" (20cm) each of plain or lightly patterned fabrics in different shades: 2 x yellow, 2 x orange, 2 x salmon pink, 2 x purple, 4 x red for the squares in the tulip fields
- 10" (25cm) each in similar shades to the above: 1 x yellow, 1 x orange, 1 x salmon pink, 1 x purple, 2 x red for the two-piece blocks in the tulip fields
- 10" (25cm) each of 6 plain fabrics of similar mid- to dark green shades for the grass between the tulip fields
- 39"(1m) natural white fabric for the white tulips and the windmills
- 1½ yd. (1.4m) black fabric for the windmills and the border

Other materials

- 87" x 71" (220 x 180cm) backing fabric
- 87" x 71" (220 x 180cm) batting
- 8¼ yd. (7.5m) red bias tape for the binding
- multicolored quilting thread

Cutting guide

10" (25cm) fabric, cut from selvage to selvage, is enough to make twenty 4¾" x 4" (12 x 10cm) rectangles. 8" (20cm) fabric is enough to make twenty 3½"(9cm) squares.

■ Method
240 two-piece blocks with green fabric

(Lesson 1: Strips, squares, triangles and Lesson 2: Two-piece blocks)
Cut forty 4¾" x 4" (12 x 10cm) rectangles from a variety of green fabrics and 40 from a variety of the other colors. Place 2 rectangles of different colored fabrics together horizontally on the cutting mat, both right sides up. Make a diagonal cut approximately down the center of both pieces of fabric. Swap over the colors and join the 2 different halves of fabric. Change the cutting angle slightly each time so that the two-piece blocks are as irregular as possible. Press the seams toward the green fabric side and trim all the blocks to make exact squares; ours were 3½" x 3½" (9 x 9cm).

280 squares

Cut exact 3½" (9cm) squares from appropriate colors for the squares in the tulip fields: you can use all the 8" (20cm)-wide strips of fabric for this.

10 windmills

Cut twenty 4¾" x 4" (12 x 10cm) rectangles each from the white and black fabrics. Make up two-piece blocks as described above. Press the seams toward the black fabric side and trim all the blocks to make exact squares; ours were 3½" x 3½" (9 x 9cm).

Sewing plan

Lay out 26 horizontal rows of 21 blocks to make the front panel, following the photo or using another arrangement if you prefer. Start, for example, with a yellow square top left and place a yellow-and-green square to the right and below it respectively, with the green section at the bottom.

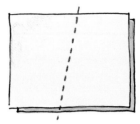

Place 2 different colored rectangles (4¾" x 4" [12 x 10cm]) of fabric together, both right sides up. Cut down the center at a slight angle, varying the cutting angle slightly with subsequent pieces.

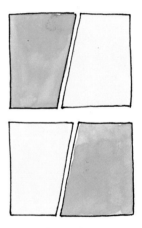

Swap over the colors and join up. Trim to make exact squares (3½" x 3½" [9 x 9cm]).

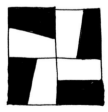

Make 10 windmills using 4 two-piece blocks in white and black for each.

Join red-and-green squares to these with the green to the left, making a zigzag line with the yellow-and-green blocks. Join 2 red squares and add more red-and-green ones, again with the green at the bottom. Use this method to make up the entire front panel, following the color sequence: yellow, red, salmon pink, yellow/white, purple, red, white/orange, yellow/white, red, salmon pink, purple, red. This arrangement has wide (2 plain squares-wide) and narrow (1 plain square-wide) fields. Arrange 3 windmills, each made from 4 black-and-white two-piece blocks, on the front. Place 2 windmills side by side on the bottom row on the right, and 5 adjacent windmills on the right-hand edge. You will have to improvise in the bottom right-hand corner, filling the corner with 4 plain squares. You could also make 2 extra two-color squares from scraps (we made 2 squares in green/purple). You will also have a few squares and two-color blocks left over.

Assembly

(Lesson 10)

Make up the front panel following the instructions for assembling blocks of equal size.

Adding the border

(Lesson 11)

Sew a 3½" (9cm)-wide strip of plain black around all the edges, making 4 red corner sections, 3½" (9cm square).

Making up the quilt and quilting

(Lessons 12 and 13)

Place the backing, batting, and pressed front panel on top of one another. Quilt branches onto the edges and orange segments on the squares in the center. A diagonal grid would be a suitable pattern for hand quilting.

Binding

(Lesson 14)

Bind the quilt with red bias tape.

Sewing plan and edging design.

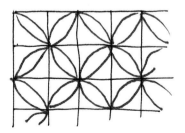

Quilting suggestion.

Grand Prismatic Spring
78¾" x 67" (200 x 170 cm)

The vivid colors of this hot spring in the Yellowstone National Park have made it world famous. The deep hues of batik fabrics are perfect for depicting the water and sulfur crystals at the pool's edge, surrounded by brown and gray rocks.

■ Materials
Fabrics
- 8" (20cm) each of 12 different batik fabrics in brown, gray, chestnut, sand, etc., for the upper area
- 8" (20cm) each of 24 different batik fabrics in the colors of the rainbow for the shoreline and the water, e.g. maroon, purple, blue, aquamarine, turquoise, lime green, lemon yellow, deep yellow, amber
- 24" (60cm) plain black fabric for the border triangles
- 39"(1m) gray-black striped fabric for the binding

Other materials
- 87" x 75" (220 x 190cm) backing fabric
- 87" x 75" (220 x 190cm) batting
- quilting thread in brown, yellow, green, blue, and black

Cutting guide
4" (10cm) fabric, cut from selvage to selvage, is enough to make eight 4¾" x 4" (12 x 10cm) rectangles.

■ Method
(Lesson 1: Strips, squares, triangles and Lesson 2: Two-piece blocks)
Sort the fabrics by color, following the photo. Don't forget the grays when you are grouping the colors for the upper part of the quilt. Cut 16 rectangles approx. 4¾" x 4" (12 x 10cm) in each color. Pin the rectangles in each color together as you work, using one pin for each. Arrange the piles of rectangles in the correct color order.

Lay 2 rectangles in adjacent colors, one on top of the other, lengthways on the cutting mat, right sides up. Cut both fabrics at a slight angle approximately down the center. Vary the cutting angle for subsequent blocks slightly to make them as irregular as possible. Swap over the colors. Join up the 2 different halves of fabric.

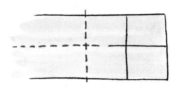

Dividing an 8" (20cm)-wide strip of fabric into rectangles.

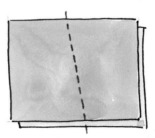

Place 2 different colored rectangles (4¾" x 4" [12 x 10cm]) of fabric together, both right sides up. Cut down the center at a slight angle, varying the cutting angle slightly with subsequent pieces.

Press and cut each block to an exact square; ours were 3½" x 3½" (9 x 9cm). Pin together the 16 blocks of each color combination, keeping the blocks in the correct color sequence.

68 edge triangles
Cut the black fabric into 17 squares at exactly 6¾" x 6¾" (17 x 17cm) and divide these twice diagonally to make 68 triangles with the straight grain running along the long edge. Use 4 of these triangles for the corners.

Swap over the colors and join up. Trim to make exact squares (3½" x 3½" [9 x 9cm]).

Divide the black fabric squares (6¾" x 6¾" [17 x 17cm]) twice diagonally to make the border triangles.

Sewing plan

Find a space large enough for laying out the complete quilt. Starting at the bottom edge with maroon and purple, arrange the blocks diagonally, beginning at a corner. Lay out the 1st row so that the center seam of the block runs from bottom left to top right. Arrange the 2nd row so that the center seam runs from bottom right to top left and the blocks fill the gaps in the 1st row. The 3rd row is arranged as the 1st row, with the color at the bottom of the blocks matching the color at the top of the blocks on the previous row. An arrangement like this of 2 identical or very similar fabrics will create a zigzag line. The color sequence is: A/B – B/C – C/D – D/E – E/F – F/G, and so on.

Lay out 35 horizontal rows, creating 3 continuous gray zigzag lines in the top area of the quilt (see photo).

To ensure the front panel of the quilt always ends with a complete block at each side, alternate long rows (16 blocks) and short rows (15 blocks), leaving out the last block on one side on every other row. The top and bottom rows of the quilt should each be 16 blocks wide.

Place the black triangles in the gaps at the edges, with their long sides facing out. Place a triangle at each of the 4 corners with their long sides adjacent to the corner square. These triangles will be a little too large for the corners, so trim their outside edges to fit.

Assembly

(Lesson 10)

Join up the quilt front panel in diagonal rows, following the instructions for assembling blocks of equal size. Starting at the top left corner, join 2 rows of blocks to make a double row. Add the black border triangles at each end of the rows.

Making up the quilt and quilting

(Lessons 12 and 13)

Place the backing, batting, and pressed front panel on top of one another. Using a chalk pencil, draw parallel curved lines in the shape of a rainbow, freehand across the front of the quilt. Quilt along these lines either by hand or using your sewing machine.

Binding

(Lesson 14)

Cut 2½" (6cm)-wide strips of gray-and-black striped fabric on the bias. Join strips to make a piece long enough to go around the edge the quilt. Fold in half legthways and use to bind the quilt.

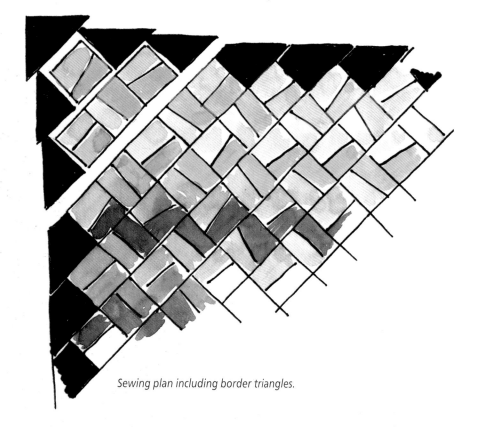

Sewing plan including border triangles.

Quarry Face
90½" x 75" (230 x 190cm)

A disused quarry is an ideal location for paragliding. The idea for this quilt came as we drove past the quarry at Dossenheim in Germany, where paragliders hover in the air beneath their brightly colored wings when the weather is fine.

■ Materials
Fabrics

- 10" (25cm) each of 10 different light sand-colored fabrics, plain or delicately patterned
- 10" (25cm) each of 10 different mid-brown and sand-colored fabrics
- 10" (25cm) each of 10 different darker brown and sand-colored fabrics
- 10" (25cm) each of 8 different plain light to mid-green fabrics, delicately patterned with leaf and grass patterns for the foliage
- 5" (12cm) each of 4 different dark green fabrics or suitable scraps for the bottom row of foliage
- 20" (50cm) plain light blue fabric for the sky
- 5 scraps of fabric approx. 10" (25cm) square in red, purple, and blue and 5 scraps of the same size in matching darker tones for the parachutes
- 8" (20cm) yellow fabric for the piped edges of the parachutes
- scrap of fabric approx. 4" x 8" (10 x 20cm) deep purple for the paragliders

Other materials

- 99" x 83" (250 x 210cm) backing fabric
- 99" x 83" (250 x 210cm) batting
- quilting thread in beige, light brown, light blue, and green
- 3¾ yd. (2.50m) bias tape in light blue for the binding at the top
- 6½ yd. (6m) bias tape in light olive green for the remaining binding

Cutting guide

10" (25cm) sand-colored fabric, cut from selvage to selvage, is enough to make 2 quarry blocks. 5" (12cm) green fabric, cut from selvage to selvage, is enough to make 9 blocks of foliage.

■ Method
49 Quarry blocks

(Lesson 5: Working with strips)
Cut strips of 1¼"–2½" (3–6cm) from the different shades of brown, keeping them sorted into piles of light/medium/dark fabrics. Leave a scrap of approx. 5" (12cm) of each of the fabrics to make the

Starting at the selvage edge, cut strips of different widths from a 10" (25cm) piece of fabric (long quarter).

Join up a variety of different brown strips to make a block. Press and cut to size (ours were 9" [23cm] high and 11¾" [30cm] wide).

four-piece blocks in the foliage rows. Set aside approx. 60 of the strips to make the foliage steps.

Make some strip sections as described in Lesson 5: sew some strips together along their long sides, using as many as are required to make a block approx. 12"–13" (30–33cm) wide. Trim all the blocks to the same size; ours were 9" (23cm) high and 11¾" (30cm) wide.

250 Foliage blocks

(Lesson 3: Four-piece blocks)
Cut pieces approx. 4¾" (12cm) square.
You will need:
Blue: approx. 10 squares
Green: approx. 220 squares
Brown: approx. 60 squares

11 x block A = 1 blue/ 3 different greens.

6 x block B = 3 different blues/1 green.

140 x block C = 4 different greens.

80 x block D = 1 brown/ 3 different greens.

60 x block E = 3 different browns/1 green.

Keeping the brown fabrics sorted into light/medium/dark, make four-piece blocks in different color combinations. Make more blocks than the minimum required so you can mix up the colors well. You will need:

11 x block A = 1 blue/3 different greens
6 x block B = 3 different blues/1 green
140 x block C = 4 different greens
80 x block D = 1 brown/3 different greens
60 x block E = 3 different browns/1 green

Trim all the four-piece blocks to an exact square; ours were exactly 3½" x 3½" (9 x 9cm).

5 foliage step blocks

Use the sand-colored strips you set aside to make narrow blocks just over 3½" (9cm) wide. Trim all the blocks to exactly 3½" (9cm) wide, to match the width of the green four-piece blocks. For each set of steps use 4 x block C (4 different greens).

Place the 4 foliage blocks in an ascending row on the cutting mat and place a sand-colored strip section above each block. Cut across all 4 strip sections at a height of approx. 8" (20cm) (measured from the lower edge of the strips). Place the pieces you have removed from the top to fill the

gaps at the bottom of the green four-piece blocks. To break up the outline of the foliage steps a little, you can "smooth out" some of the corners. Cut a corner from the sand-colored strip section you have selected and replace it with a triangle of green fabric. You can make these by cutting a green 10" (25cm) square along its 2 diagonals. Sew on the triangle, fold out, and press. Neaten the seam allowances. Join the four-piece blocks

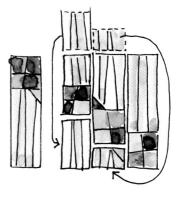

Foliage step blocks: lay out 4 green foliage blocks in an ascending row on the cutting mat. Join up several sand-colored strips until they are as wide as a foliage block. Join a strip section to the top edge of each foliage block. Cut off the excess strip sections at the top and use these to fill the gaps at the bottom. You may like to add some green triangular corners first.

Finished foliage step blocks: join a row of four-piece foliage blocks to the top.

and the strip sections and press the seam allowances toward the green side. Join up the 4 sections along their long sides and press. Join 4 foliage blocks together and then join this strip to the top edge of the step block. Trim each completed foliage step block to exactly 11¾" x 11¾" (30 x 30cm). Make a total of 4 sets of steps running from top left to bottom right and 1 set running from top right to bottom left.

Sewing plan

Using the photo as a guide, sort the quarry blocks from light to dark and arrange on your pin board. Start with 7 light blocks in the first row and arrange the other rows with the colors getting darker as you go down. The darkest blocks should be saved for the eighth row. Place the foliage step blocks as in the photo.

The top row that includes some blue sky is made using the blue and green foliage blocks (blocks A and B). Fill up any gaps with blue fabric. Arrange 4 foliage blocks (blocks C, D, and E) along the top edge of each quarry block so that the green edge is next to the quarry block.

Join the 4 foliage blocks together and then join this strip to the top edge of each quarry block. Use the darker tone foliage blocks toward the bottom of the quilt. Press the seam allowances toward the green side and trim each block to exactly 11¾" x 11¾" (30 x 30cm).

Assembly

(Lesson 10)

First, join up the blocks to make horizontal rows. Trim the bottom edge of the 2 top quarry face rows by 4" (10cm) each and the next 2 by 2" (5cm). This will give the image perspective and will shorten the quilt, which is otherwise likely to turn out to be too long.

Join up the horizontal rows in descending order. Join a 9" (23cm)-high light blue strip running the full width of the quilt to the top edge of the first row to form the sky. Don't worry about the little seam.

The bottom row is made up of a double layer of dark green four-piece blocks. "Soften" the top edge of the strip with the occasional lighter green or brown section, This will give the quilt visual weight.

Note

Block dimensions of 11¾" x 11¾" (30 x 30cm) are used for this design. If your work turns out to be a different size, don't change it. The idea for the slightly shorter upper rows of the quarry face only came to us when everything had already been sewn up, so we shortened both these rows afterward. We found a use for the bits we cut off in Desert roses (page 49).

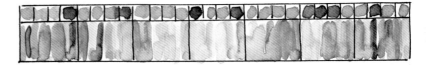

A row of the quilt: shorten rows 1 and 2 by about 4" (10cm) at the bottom; shorten rows 3 and 4 by about 2" (5cm) at the bottom. The lower rows should be darker than the upper ones—bear this in mind when sorting the colors.

Join a row of 4 foliage blocks to the top edge of the quarry blocks. Press and trim to a square (ours were 11¾" x 11¾" [30 x 30cm]).

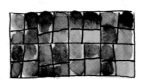

Bottom row: double layer of four-piece dark green blocks (ours were 11¾" [30cm] square).

Making up the quilt and quilting
(Lessons 12 and 13)
Lay the backing, batting, and pressed front panel on top of one another. Using the appropriate colors, quilt meanders in the sky, leaf shapes onto the green foliage blocks and small green sections, and vertical lines at irregular intervals onto the quarry blocks. Quilt vertical leaf shapes onto the bottom dark green section.

Binding
(Lesson 14)
Bind the basted quilt edge with light blue bias tape around the sky and light olive-green bias tape for the other edges.

Quilting suggestion for the quarry face; a sample block.

Quilting suggestion for the bottom section; a sample block.

Paragliders
(Lesson 8: Piping techniques)
If you like, you can appliqué a few paragliders of different sizes onto the quilt. I used a machine-sewn appliqué technique that is turned right side out.

Enlarge the templates below or design 3 paragliders of different sizes traveling in different directions. Trace the templates onto paper and cut out the pieces. Decide which look better at the bottom and which at the top.

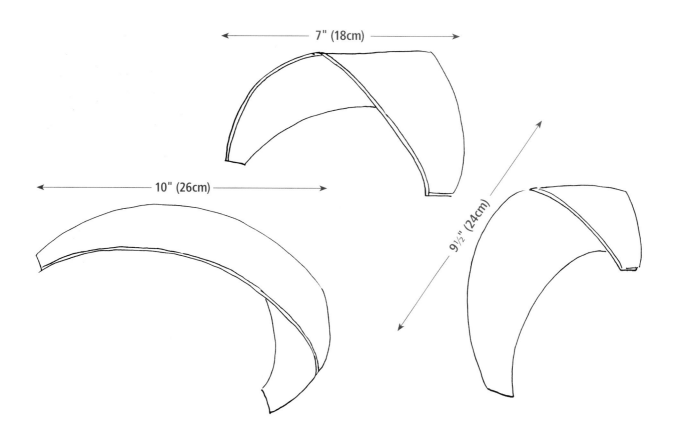

7" (18cm)

10" (26cm)

9½" (24cm)

The lower part of the parachute is a darker shade and should be made first. The upper part is lighter and will overlap the adjoining edge of the darker section when appliquéd.

Dark parachute underside piece: place a piece of yellow piping fabric and a piece of deep purple fabric together, right sides facing, and pin together. Trace around the appropriate part of the template onto the piping fabric. Sew around the outer edges of the piece leaving the short seam open. Cut out the piece, leaving a seam allowance and adding approx. ½" (1cm) at the short seam edge (this will be hidden under the top side, which will lie on top of it). Turn the section inside out through the open edge. Push the piping fabric about ¹⁄₁₆" (1–2mm) round to the front edge of the parachute so it is visible as a colored edge. Press.

Light parachute upper piece: place a piece of yellow piping fabric and a piece of colored fabric (e.g. red) together, right sides facing, and pin. Trace around the appropriate part of the template onto the piping fabric. Sew around the outer edges of the piece. Cut out the piece, leaving seam allowances. Clip around the seam allowances and make an approx. 2–2½" (5–6cm)-long opening in the center of the piping fabric. Turn the section inside out through this opening. Push the piping fabric about ¹⁄₁₆" (1–2mm) round to the front edge of the parachute so it is visible as a colored edge. Press. Pin the darker underside piece of the parachute to the quilt. Align the upper piece on top, overlapping the open edge of the underside. Appliqué the parachute

around the edge using a sewing machine or appliqué with blind stitches along the edges by hand. The paragliders should not be quilted. Add a dark rectangle as a "pilot" underneath in the parachute. To make this, fold back and press the edges of a rectangle of fabric about 1¼" (3cm) wide and appliqué the edges by hand; you don't need to show the parachute cords.

Cut out the piece, including a seam allowance. Clip the seam allowance and cut an opening in the piping fabric.

Turn the shape inside out through the opening, pushing the piping to the front.

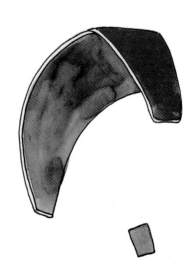

Appliqué the lower paraglider section first, then appliqué the upper part to overlap. Appliqué a dark rectangle below the parachute as a "pilot."

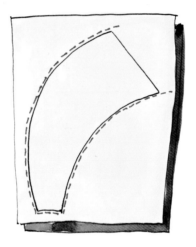

Parachute, underside piece: place parachute and piping fabric together with right sides facing. Trace the shape around the template and sew around the edges of the shape, leaving the short seam open.

Parachute, upper piece: place the parachute and piping fabrics together with right sides facing. Trace the shape around the template and sew around it.

Flower Carpet
61" x 49¼" (155 x 125cm)

There are some magnificent fabrics that I just can't resist. The red here stands out beautifully against the unbleached cotton.

■ Materials
Fabrics

- 4" (10cm) each of 7 or 8 different floral fabrics with plenty of green for the center blocks and background insets
- 1¾ yd. (1.50m) natural white cotton or unbleached calico for the background and the edge triangles
- 2¼ yd. (2m) large-patterned floral fabric in shades of red, orange, and pink for the flowerbeds, for parts of the center blocks, and for the outer border
- 24" (60cm) plain black fabric for the flowerbed rows
- 8" (20cm) black-and-white striped (stripe width approx. ½" [1cm]) for the inner border

Other materials

- 70" x 59" (170 x 150cm) backing fabric
- 70" x 59" (170 x 150cm) batting
- 6¼ yd. (5.70m) red bias tape
- quilting thread in red and offwhite

■ Method
Preparation

Cut four 6" (15cm)-wide strips from the red large-patterned floral fabric for the outer border (2 approx. 70" [170cm] long, 2 approx. 60" [150cm] long) and set aside. Cut down the fabric lengthways so there are no joined seams.

86 four-piece blocks

(Lesson 3: Four-piece blocks)
Cut 86 approx. 4" (10cm) squares from the assorted green floral fabrics. Make up four-piece blocks using 4 different fabrics each time, as described in Lesson 3. Trim back any excess at the edges. Set 14 blocks aside for the background insets. Join 4 four-piece blocks to make a square and repeat with the remainder. Trim all the blocks to the same size; ours were 5" x 5" (13 x 13cm). You will need 18 multicolor four-piece blocks for the center blocks.

Make 86 four-piece blocks from approx. 4" (10cm) squares of different colorful floral fabrics. Set aside 14 of these blocks.

Using 4 x four-piece blocks, make 18 center blocks, then cut to an exact square (5" x 5" [13 x 13cm]).

18 flowerbed blocks

Cut the remaining red large-floral fabric into two 40" (1m)-long pieces. Cutting along the length of these pieces, cut strips approx. 8" (20cm) wide. Working freehand without a ruler, cut the strips lengthways into three or four narrow strips. Make the outside strips slightly wider than the inner strips. Cut ¾" (2cm)-wide strips of black fabric and insert a black strip between each of the long strips. Press the seam allowances toward the red fabric sides.

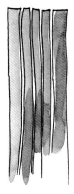

Cut the large-patterned floral fabric into approx. 8" (20cm)-wide strips and make three or four lengthways cuts.

Insert approx. ¾" (2cm)-wide black strips into the cuts. Cut off sections about 3½"–4" (9–10cm) high.

From these completed strips, cut 72 smaller sections approx. 3½–4" (9–10cm) high. Trim to exactly 5" (13cm) wide (the width of the center blocks).

Cut 72 squares approx. 4" x 4" (10 x 10cm) from the natural white cotton for the corner pieces. Join 1 red flowerbed block to the upper and lower edge of each center block; make 18 of these blocks in total. Join a white square to the short ends of 36 red flowerbed blocks and join one of these sections to either side of the center

Join a white cotton square to the sides of the 36 red flowerbed blocks.

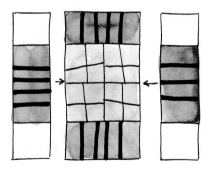

Join a red flowerbed block to the top and bottom edges of each center block. Now add 2 sections from the previous step to the right- and left-hand sides. Press the block and trim to an exact square (10" x 10" [25 x 25cm]).

blocks. Trim the 18 completed blocks to the same size; ours were exactly 10" x 10" (25 x 25cm).

10 edge triangles and 4 corner triangles

Using the natural white cotton, cut seven 2" (5cm)-wide strips from selvage to selvage. Cut 7 squares of approx. 7" x 7" (18 x 18cm) and divide each twice diagonally to make a total of 28 triangles. Using the 14 four-piece blocks that were previously set aside, join 2 triangles to each one as shown in the diagram. Trim off the excess fabric at the corner of the first triangle before sewing on the second, always starting the seam at the four-piece block. Press these sections and set 4 aside for the 4 corner triangles.

Join the 2" (5cm)-wide strips to the edges of the remaining four-piece blocks, always starting the seam at the four-piece block. Unfold the first strip and trim the end in line with the long edge of the triangular section. Join the second strip, again trimming the end in line with the edge of the triangular section. Press the blocks. Check that all the blocks form a right angle, trimming where necessary; use a large square ruler for this or use the grid lines of the cutting mat as a guide.

Sewing plan

Arrange the blocks on the diagonal. Start with 3 blocks in the top row and add another 6 horizontal rows in order beneath. Add the 4 small corner triangles, placing the colored four-piece block at the outside corner. Arrange the edge triangles into the gaps along the border.

Cut 7" (18cm) squares of white cotton down both diagonals to make 4 triangles. Join a triangle to the edge of a four-piece block. Trim off any excess fabric at the corner to align.

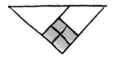

Join a second triangle to the adjacent edge of the four-piece block. Set aside 4 of these sections for the corners.

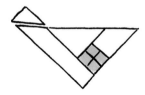

Join a 2" (5cm)-wide white cotton strip to the remaining 10 sections. Trim off the excess ends in line with the long edge of the triangle.

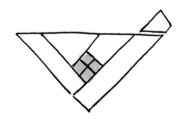

Join a strip to the other edge in the same way. Press and trim.

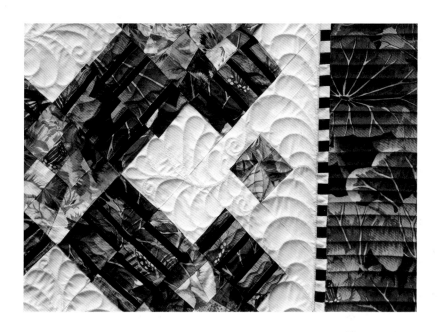

Assembly

(Lesson 10)

Assemble the quilt front panel. Trim the outer edges so they are straight.

Adding the border

(Lesson 11)

Join the 2 border sections to the center panel.

Inner border: black-and-white striped fabric cut into 1¼" (3cm) strips, straight corners.

Outer border: red large-patterned floral fabric, cut into 6" (15cm) strips, mitered corners.

Making up the quilt and quilting

(Lessons 12 and 13)

Lay the backing, batting and pressed front panel on top of one another. Quilt a flame pattern onto the red fabrics with red thread and stitch round the four-piece squares so they puff out like small pillows. Quilt an ornate feather pattern onto the natural white background areas and simple stripes onto the border.

Binding

(Lesson 14)

Bind the basted edge with red bias tape.

Border design and quilting suggestion.

Spruce Plantation
94½" x 78¾" (240 x 200cm)

An all-green design can never be boring. This quilt represents a plantation of young fir trees, fenced in to protect them from wild animals. The trees stand out against the heavily quilted leaf-pattern background.

■ Materials
Fabrics
- 8" (20cm) each of 18 different light green fabrics, from lime and grass green to light olive, plain, and lightly patterned, for the trees
- 8" (20cm) each of 18 different dark green fabrics, from blue-green to pine green and dark olive, plain, and lightly patterned, for the trees
- 4" (10cm) each of 3 different mid-brown to red-brown fabrics for the tree trunks
- Scrap of red fabric cut into four 2" x 2" (5 x 5cm) squares for the corners of the accent border
- 6" (15cm) each of plain white and black fabrics for the accent border

Other materials
- 103" x 87" (260 x 220cm) backing fabric
- 103" x 87" (260 x 220cm) batting
- 10 yd. (9.20m) red bias tape for the binding
- variegated quilting thread in shades of green

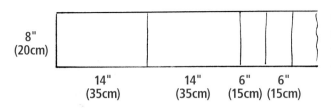

Suggested division of an 8" (20cm)-wide strip of fabric, cut from selvage to selvage.

Cutting guide
8" (20cm) green fabric, cut from selvage to selvage, is enough for 2 large and 2 small trees. Suggested division of an 8" (20cm)-wide strip: 14"/14"/6"/6" (35cm/35m/15m/15cm). Keep the scraps to fill any gaps.

■ Method
92 large tree blocks
(Lesson 1: Strips, squares, triangles and Lesson 4: Narrow triangles)
Cut thirty-one 8" x 14" (20 x 35cm) rectangles from both the light and dark green fabrics. Cut some brown strips approximately 1¼" (3cm) wide for the tree trunks. Place a light rectangle on top of a dark rectangle vertically on the cutting mat, both with right sides facing upward. Make a horizontal cut about 2"–2½" (5–6cm) up from the bottom edge to allow for the tree trunk. Place the rotary cutter approx. 1¼" (3cm) in from the right-hand bottom corner of the larger piece of fabric and cut diagonally to the center top. Move the two pieces of fabric slightly apart. Starting 1¼" (3cm) in from the left-hand bottom corner, now cut diagonally upward to approx. 1¼"–1½" (3–4cm) below the top edge.

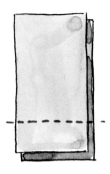

Place 2 green rectangles together, both right sides up, and cut off a 1½"–2" (4–5cm)-wide strip from the bottom.

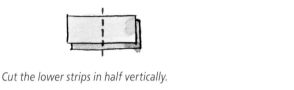

Cut the lower strips in half vertically.

Insert an approx. 1¼" (3cm)-wide strip for a tree trunk.

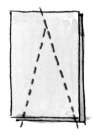

Cut triangular pieces from the rectangles by making one long and one short cut through both layers of fabric.

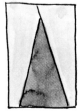 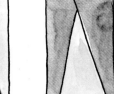

Swap over the colors.

Join the left-hand side of the triangle to the background piece; trim off the excess seam allowance at the top.

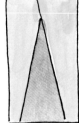

Join the right-hand background piece.

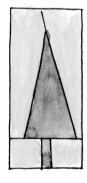

Join the lower section with the tree trunk to the tree piece. Press and trim all the blocks to a uniform size. Make 92 large tree blocks.

Make 77 small tree blocks.

Swap over the colors. Cut the lower strips in half vertically and insert an approx. 1¼" (3cm)-wide tree trunk of the same height as the strip of green fabric. Now make the tree. Begin by joining the left-hand side of the triangle to the background piece. Press the seam allowance to the tree side. Trim off the excess seam allowance at the top and join the right-hand background piece. Finally, join the lower strip, making sure the tree trunk is centered under the tree. Press all the blocks and trim them to the same size; ours were 6" (15cm) wide and 11¾" (30cm) high.

77 small tree blocks
Cut thirty-nine 8" x 6" (20 x 15cm) triangles from both the light green and the dark green fabrics. Make 78 small blocks using the same method described for the large blocks. The tree trunks will be approx. ¾"–1¼" (2–3cm) wide and 1½"–2" (4–5cm) high. Press all the blocks and trim them to the same size; ours were 4¼" (11cm) wide and 6¾" (17cm) high.

Accent border
(Lesson 9)
Make a strip approx. 5½ yd. (5m) long from the 2" (5cm)-wide white and black strips for the accent border. Put aside four 2" x 2" (5 x 5cm) red squares for the corner pieces.

Sewing plan

Arrange the small tree blocks in 8 horizontal rows of 9 blocks each. Alternate light and dark trees and mix up the different shades as much as possible. Join up the pieces to make section A (Lesson 10). Add the accent border around section A. Make sure the border strip has a white square at the beginning and the end. Make some of the seams narrower or wider if need be, to ensure that everything is the right length and joins up properly. Place a red square in each corner.

To make the side sections B and C, join 4 horizontal rows of 4 large tree blocks for each section. The lengths of these sections may serendipitously match the sides of the center panel; if not, add a row of small trees or sew green fabric scraps together in a random order and trim them to the correct width and height. In our quilt, the large tree blocks were shortened slightly from the top in the right-hand section C so that a row of small trees made of 5 blocks fitted along the bottom edge. A row made up of green scraps was sewn along the top edge of the left-hand section B. Join sections B and C to the sides of center section A.

To make sections D and E, arrange 2 horizontal rows of 15 large trees at the top and bottom, paying attention to the sequence of colors. Join up the sections. To ensure the seams of the top and center sections line up exactly, you may have to make some pieces wider or narrower; be sure to do this around the accent border.

Making up the quilt and quilting
(Lessons 12 and 13)

Lay the backing, batting, and pressed front panel on top of one another. Machine quilting: Cover the background of the large trees with a dense leaf pattern and quilt along the seams of the small tree blocks without touching the trees.
Hand quilting: quilt the contours of the trees.

Binding
(Lesson 14)

Bind the quilt with red bias tape.

Sewing plan: make up center panel A and edge with the accent border. Make up sections B and C and place level with center panel A. Join sections B and C to the right- and left-hand sides of A and then join sections D and E to the top and bottom respectively.

Quilting suggestion: densely packed leaf pattern.

Limestone Landscape
82½" x 78¾" (210 x 200cm)

The gleaming white travertine terraces at Pamukkale in Turkey have become world famous. This quilt, which literally flows over the terraces in this photo, is sewn in delicate pastel colors.

▇ Materials
Fabrics
- 5 yd. (4.50m) white fabric for the stalactites
- 5 yd. (4.50m) in total of 3 or more different light gray fabrics, plain or lightly patterned, for the shadows
- 1¼ yd. (1m) each of turquoise and light turquoise fabric for the pools of water
- 16" (40cm) pink or pink-and-white striped fabric for the inner border
- 1½ yd. (1.20m) pale lime-green fabric for the outer border

Other materials
- 91" x 87" (230 x 220cm) backing fabric
- 91" x 87" (230 x 220cm) batting
- 9 yd. (8.30m) lemon-yellow bias tape for the binding
- quilting thread in very light blue or light gray

▇ Method
330 stalactites
(Lesson 1: Strips, squares, triangles and Lesson 4: Narrow triangles)
Cut 165 rectangles of approx. 4" x 10" (10 x 25cm) from the white fabric and 165 rectangles from the assorted light gray fabrics. Place a white and a gray rectangle

together lengthways on the cutting mat, both right sides up. Place the rotary cutter approx. ½" (1cm) in from the bottom right corner and cut diagonally up toward the center top. Slide the pieces of fabric apart a little. Starting ½" (1cm) in from the bottom left corner, make a cut to meet the first cut approx. 1¼"–1½" (3–4cm) down from the top edge.

Swap over the colors and join up. Start by sewing the shorter seam from the lower edge of the fabric. Press the seam allowance toward the inset long triangle. Trim the excess fabric of the background piece and join on the opposite background piece. Press the seam allowance in the same direction as the first. Press all the blocks and cut them to exactly the same width; ours were 2½" (6cm).

66 stalactite blocks
Make up the stalactites in sections. Arrange 5 of the stalactites in an arc on the cutting mat as shown in the diagram; the white fabric should always be at the top and the gray at the bottom. Join up the long edges of the pieces. The white stalactites in the 33 x block A will have a center seam; the 33 x block B will have a center seam in the gray shadow.

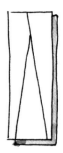

Place a white and gray rectangle together, both right sides up. Make a triangle shape with a long and a short cut through both layers.

Swap over the colors and join the pieces. Press and cut all the blocks to the same width (ours were 2½" [6cm]).

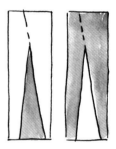

33 x block A: groups of 5 triangles with the center seams in the white fabrics.

33 x block B: groups of 5 triangles with the center seams in the gray fabrics.

Pools of water

(Lesson 6: Curved seams)

Cut 44 turquoise rectangles of approx. 10" x 2½" (25 x 6cm), 12 turquoise rectangles of approx. 10" x 4" (25 x 10cm) and 11 white rectangles of approx. 10" x 4" (25 x 10cm).

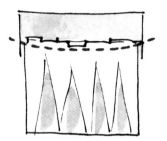

Place a turquoise rectangle behind the top edge of the stalactite block and make a curved cut through both layers.

Place one of the turquoise (or white) rectangles lengthways on the cutting mat and place one of the stalactite blocks on top, both fabrics right sides up. The lowest point of the stalactite block should just overlap the bottom edge of the turquoise (or white) rectangle. Using a rotary cutter,

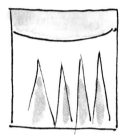

Join the turquoise piece to the top edge of the stalactite block with a curved seam.

cut the top edge of the stalactite blocks freehand into an arc through both layers of fabric. Discard the excess pieces of fabric.

To make the double-width pools of water, place 2 A blocks and 2 turquoise rectangles side by side and cut the arc across both blocks.

Join the turquoise pieces to the stalactite blocks with a curved seam. Press the seam allowance toward the turquoise side. Trim all the blocks to the same width with straight top and bottom edges so that all the corners are all at right angles. They can be different heights.

Sewing plan

(Lesson 10)

Arrange the blocks in 8 vertical rows of 8 blocks each. Follow the sewing plan or use your own arrangement if you prefer. Arrange the blocks at irregular intervals to mimic the natural arrangements of pools of water. Make sure that the double-width pools of water line up exactly by moving or shortening the neighboring blocks where necessary. You can extend the top and/or bottom edge of the rows with smaller blocks or pieces of white fabric.

Row A: join blocks A1 to A8 to make section A.

Rows B/C: join blocks B1 to B3 to make a section and repeat with blocks B4 to B5, then join the long sides of both B sections to make a double row.

Join blocks C1 to C5 and C6 to C10, then join the long sides of both C sections to make a double row.

Join section B and section C.

Row D: Join blocks D1 to D8 to make section D.

Rows E/F: join blocks E1 to E5 and E6 to E10, then join the long sides of both E sections to make a double row.

Join blocks F1 to F3 and F4 to F6, then join the long sides of both F sections to make a double row.

Rows G/H/I: join blocks G1 to G4 and G5 to G9, then join the long sides of both G sections to make a double row.

Join blocks H1 to H3 and H4 to H6, then join the long sides of both H sections to make a double row. Join the sides of blocks I1 and I2. Join sections G, H and I.

Close up the long seams between the rows and trim the bottom edge of the quilt panel so it is straight.

Adding the border
(Lesson 11)
Inner border: pink-and-white striped fabric, cut to 2" (5cm) strips, straight corners.
Outer border: pale lime-green fabric, cut to 5" (13cm) strips, straight corners.

Making up the quilt and quilting
(Lessons 12 and 13)
Lay the backing, batting, and pressed front panel one on top of the other.

Suggestion for machine quilting: cover the gray triangles with a dense vertical zigzag pattern, leaving the white stalactites untouched so they stand slightly proud. Using light blue thread, quilt water streaks onto the turquoise areas. Work a decorative agave-leaf pattern onto the lime- green border, covering the gaps with a dense pattern (stippling). Quilt along the seams of the pink border.

Suggestion for hand quilting: quilt the gray triangles in the seams or along the seams at a distance of a seam allowance. Quilt along the seams of the pink border and make a wave pattern on the outer border.

Binding
(Lesson 14)
Bind the quilt with lemon-yellow bias tape.

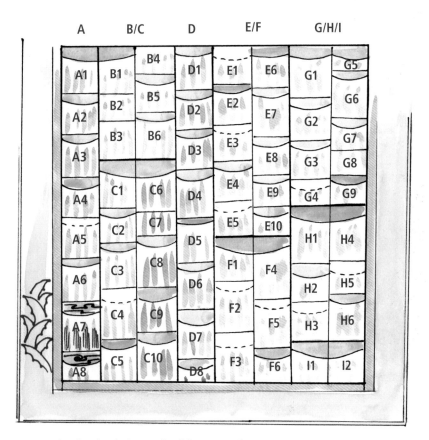

Sewing plan, border design, and quilting suggestion.

Strawberry Fields
39¼" x 34½" (100 x 88cm)

You can also make this quilt in a larger size—with rows and rows of strawberry plants. Just multiply up the fabric required. The pale straw-yellow background sets off the fruit and leaves to perfection.

■ Materials
Fabrics
- 4" (10cm) each of 3 different red fabrics for the strawberries (or an appropriate number of scraps of approx. 4" x 4" [10 x 10cm])
- 4" (10cm) each of 8 different green fabrics for the leaves and the corner sections (or an appropriate number of scraps of approx. 4" x 4" [10 x 10cm])
- 1½ yd. (1.20m) straw-colored fabric for the background and the border

Other materials
- 48" x 39" (120 x 100cm) backing fabric
- 48" x 39" (120 x 100cm) batting
- 4¼ yd. (3.80m) red bias tape
- quilting thread in beige and green

■ Method
44 x green four-piece blocks A
(Lesson 3: Four-piece blocks)
Cut 44 squares of approx. 4" x 4" (10 x 10cm) from the various green fabrics. Make 44 four-piece blocks from 4 different squares, as described in Lesson 3. Trim them all to the same size; ours were exactly 3¼" x 3¼" (8 x 8cm). Set aside 4 of these blocks for the corner sections.

48 x strawberry block B
Cut 36 different green squares and 12 different red squares of approx. 4" x 4" (10 x 10cm). Make four-piece blocks from 1 red square and 3 green squares, as described in Lesson 3. Cut them all to the same size; ours were exactly 3¼" x 3¼" (8 x 8cm).

48 x strawberry blocks C
Cut 36 straw-colored squares and 12 different red squares of approx. 4" x 4" (10 x 10cm). Make four-piece blocks from 3 straw-colored squares and 1 red square, as described in Lesson 3. Cut them all to the same size; ours were exactly 3¼" x 3¼" (8 x 8cm).

Filler pieces
Trim 8 straw-colored squares to the size of the four-piece blocks (ours were exactly 3¼" x 3¼" [8 x 8cm]). Cut 44 straw-colored rectangles of 3¼" x 2" (8 x 5cm) (approx. half the size of the four-piece blocks) for the gaps at the edge of the fields.

Block A, 4 different shades of green, make 44.

Block B, 3 green and 1 red, make 48.

Block C, 3 straw color and 1 red, make 48.

Sewing plan
Start with a center green row. To make this, arrange a row of 10 green four-piece blocks A, moving every second one up by half a block. Insert the strawberry blocks B into the gaps created. Arrange the red corners so that they face outward.

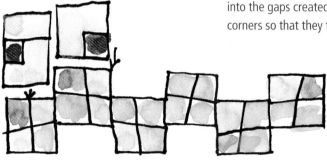

Arrange a row of 10 blocks A, placing every second one a half-block higher. Arrange the strawberry blocks to fill the gaps created.

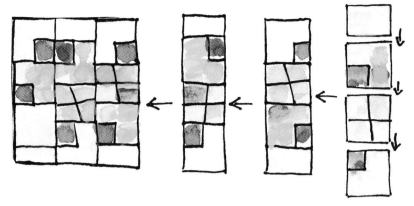

Join vertical rows of 3 half blocks each, then join up the rows to make a section. Join 4 of these strawberry sections to one another.

Border design and quilting suggestion.

Insert a strawberry block C into each of the half-block-high gaps at the top and bottom edges of the row, with the red corners at the outer edges. Fill the gaps at the top and bottom with straw-colored rectangles. Give the fields irregular ends by adding a block B and one or two blocks C.

Join the 3 half blocks to make vertical rows, then join up the rows to make a section. Trim the edges straight. Make 4 sections like this and join them to make the quilt front panel. Press the panel and trim the outer edges straight.

Adding the border
(Lesson 11)
Use strips of straw-colored 3¼" (8cm)-wide fabric (the width of the four-piece blocks), using a four-piece block A for each corner section.

Making up the quilt and quilting
(Lessons 12 and 13)
Lay the backing, batting, and pressed front panel one on top of the other. Use beige thread to quilt feathers or a meandering pattern onto the straw-colored areas and use green thread to quilt a small leaf pattern onto the green areas. Leave the red "strawberries" alone—this will make them stand out.

Binding
(Lesson 14)
Bind the basted edge with red bias tape.

STRIPS

Lesson 5:
Working with Strips
Projects: Vineyard terraces, Canyon colors, Meandering river, Quarry face

You can cut the strips from the short edge of a long quarter, either across the entire fabric width from selvage to selvage or across half the fabric width.

Cutting strips
Cut strips of fabric 1¼"–1½" (3–6cm) wide from edge to edge (lengthways or crossways) from all the fabrics in a color group; don't use a ruler when cutting but work freehand. Mix up the colors of the strips of fabric well.

Tip
If a strip section gets a bit bumpy and cannot be pressed flat, first dampen it well. Run your fingertips down one or two of the seams until the fabric lies flat, making a fold. Press the fold you have made. Sew from the wrong side along the edge of the fold and trim the (now wider) seam allowances. You might lose an interesting curved seam in the fabric, but it is more important that the strip section lies flat.

Sewing
Use the free arm of your sewing machine, if possible, so you can work with your hands as close as possible to the needle. Join up the strips, right sides together, along their long edges. To begin the seam, make a few stitches through both layers. Then hold the upper strip loosely in your left hand and the lower strip loosely in your right. Let the fabric run gently through your fingers, placing the edges of the fabric together as you continue to sew. Don't worry about seam allowances of varying widths.

Making sections
Start by making groups of two, then groups of four from two groups of two, and so on. Make the strip sections a little wider than indicated in the project instructions. Always begin and end with a slightly wider strip. Mix up the colors so that no two adjacent strips are the same color.

Pressing
Press the sections first from the wrong side, folding the seam allowances in the right direction, then from the right side to smooth out the surface, pulling the strips gently apart as you press.

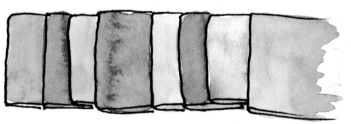

Sort fabrics into a color group and set aside.

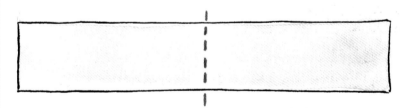

Cut a long quarter in half if necessary.

Follow the project instructions for the number and width of the strip sections you need. Cut the pieces you require from these sections.

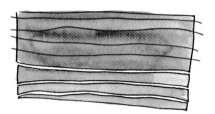

Cut strips freehand, without a ruler.

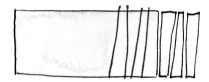

Cut the strips from the short edge of the fabric.

Mix up the fabric colors. Join the strips along their long edges, letting the fabric slide gently through your fingers and placing the edges of the fabric together as you sew.

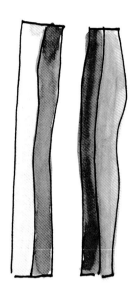

Make strip sections: first make groups of 2, then 4, and so on.

Lesson 6:
Curved Seams
Projects: Desert dwellings, Gecko pillow

Cutting curves in several layers of fabric

If you make a slightly curved cut through two or more pieces of fabric and swap over the layers, the cut edges will match exactly along the cuts you have just made.

Place two or more pieces of fabric of different colors together, all with right sides up. Cut through the fabrics. Shuffle the colors without changing the positions of the fabric pieces. To join, always place the right-hand piece of fabric over the left one, with right sides together. Start by making a few stitches to keep the pieces in place, leaving one corner of the seam allowance as excess where required (for cuts that finish at an angle on the edge). Take the uppermost piece of fabric loosely in your left hand and the lower piece in your right. Sew from top to bottom, placing the edges of the fabric together as you sew. Don't worry about seam allowances of varying widths.

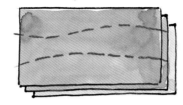

Place the fabrics together, right sides up.

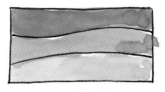

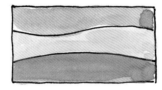

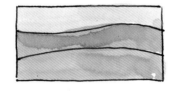

Mix up the colored layers.

Place the edges of the fabric together while sewing.

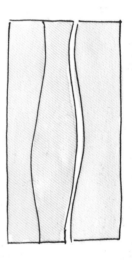

Unfold them. Lay the third piece of fabric, right sides together, over the section you have just made. Join pieces as before, press the block and trim to size.

Place the right-hand piece over the left-hand piece, right sides together. Allow the top corner of the seam allowance to overhang slightly.

Tip
When sewing curved edges, use the free arm of your sewing machine if possible; this will allow you to guide the fabric with your hands close to the needle.

Lesson 6

Joining curved edges

Projects: Wintry night, Vineyard terraces, Canyon colors

Press the piece and tidy the edges you will be working on. Lay the curved edge of this piece over the edge of the bottom section you have made, both right sides up. Cut through the lower fabric along the curved edge of the upper piece, as if you were cutting with a template; both edges will now be the same shape and the cut will run parallel. Join the edges as described above.

To ensure the long edges don't get pulled out of shape when you are joining the seam, insert 2 pins at intervals of about a handbreadth, one on each side.

When sewing the seam, make sure that these marker pins are lined up; you can always pull the fabric slightly or hold it in if you really need to.

Tidy the edge of the first piece of fabric (here, the bottom edge).

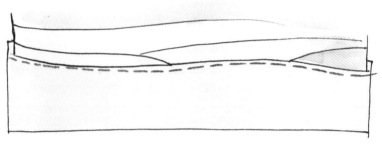

Lay the curved edge of the first piece of fabric over the bottom piece and cut along the upper edge following the curved line.

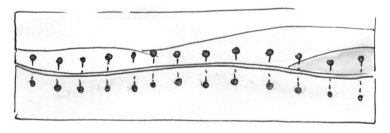

The fabric edges of both parts will now run parallel. Insert marker pins at handbreadth intervals; these should line up as you sew the seam.

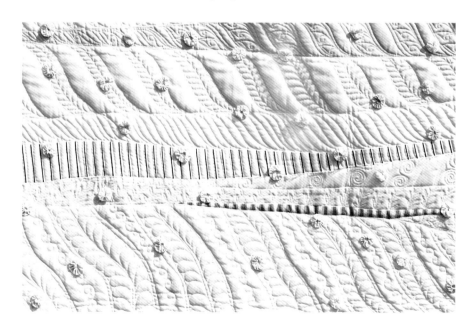

Lesson 6

Desert Roses
56" x 49¼" (142 x 125cm)

In the desert the wind forms beautiful round shapes in stone that look just like roses, so we have quilted our rose petals in sandy colors onto a background of rich desert hues. The wide border brings the center panel up to the size you need.

■ Materials

Fabrics

- 10" (25cm) each of at least 10 different sand-colored and light- brown fabrics, plain or lightly patterned, for the strips sections and the blocks C
- 10" (25cm) large-patterned floral fabric, e.g. orange and purple flowers on a light background, for the blocks A
- 2" (5cm) or a scrap of very light green fabric, plain or patterned, for the center of the sand-colored blocks B
- 4" (10cm) black-and-white striped fabric, in a strip approx. ½" (1cm) wide, for the accent border
- 1¾ yd. (1.60m) large-patterned, light, floral fabric, e.g. rose, sand or salmon pink, for the blocks D and the wide outer border

Other materials

- 63" x 59" (160 x 150cm) backing fabric
- 63" x 59" (160 x 150cm) batting
- 6 yd. (5.50m) salmon pink bias tape for the binding
- quilting thread in beige

■ Method

Preparation

Cut 12 blocks C exactly 7" x 7" (18 x 18cm) from the various sand-colored, patterned fabrics. This measurement matches the size of the trimmed blocks A.

10 strip sections

Cut 1¼"–2" (3–6cm)-wide strips from the short edges of the sand-colored and light-brown fabrics. Cut at a slight angle, so the strips are slightly wedge shaped. Join the strips along their long edges, mixing up the colors and alternating the wedge shapes so the blocks you make are straight. Join up enough strips to make a section approx. 12"–14" (30–35cm) wide. Tidy up the top and bottom edges.

From these sections, cut approx. 20 horizontal strips of approx. 2" (5cm) for blocks A and 20 horizontal strips of approx. 4" (10cm) for blocks B.

11 x block A

(Lesson 1: Strips, squares, triangles) Cut 11 squares of approx. 4¾" x 4¾" (12 x 12cm) from the heavily patterned floral fabric. Join the 2" (5cm)-wide sand-colored strips that you just made to each square, pressing the seam allowances toward the center. Trim all the blocks to the same size; ours were exactly 7" x 7" (18 x 18cm).

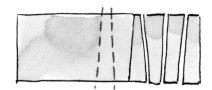

Cut the fabric into strips.

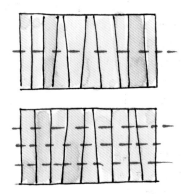

Mix up the colors and join the strips before cutting into 2" and 4" (5 and 10cm)-wide sections.

Make 11 x block A: floral center and narrow strip sections.

Make 13 x block B, green center and wide strip sections.

13 x block B

(Lesson 1: Strips, squares, triangles)
Cut squares of approx. 1¼" x 1¼"
(3 x 3cm) from the light-green fabric.
This will form the center of block B.
Add the 4" (10cm)-wide strip sections
around this central square. Press the
blocks and trim them all to the same
size; ours were exactly 7" x 7"
(18 x 18cm).

Tip

Use up all the scraps, even if it is
sometimes impossible to maintain the
usual sequence of blocks. Enlarge any
blocks that come out too small by
sewing on strips.

6 x block D: floral fabric square.

6 x rose block D and border strip

First, cut four 6" (15cm)-wide strips from
the heavily patterned, light floral fabric,
cutting along the length of the fabric, to
make the border. Then cut 6 blocks D of
exactly 7" x 7" (18 x 18cm) from the
remaining fabric.

12 x block C

These are the 12 sand-colored squares
that were cut to size and set aside
in preparation.

12 x block C: sand-colored fabric square.

Sewing plan

Arrange blocks A, B, C, and D in 7 rows of
6 blocks each; follow the plan or make
your own design if you prefer.

1st row:	C	B	C	A	B	D
2nd row:	A	A	D	C	A	C
3rd row:	B	C	A	C	B	B
4th row:	C	C	B	D	C	A
5th row:	A	B	A	B	A	D
6th row:	C	D	C	A	B	C
7th row:	B	A	B	C	D	B

Adding the border

(Lesson 11)
Accent border: black-and-white striped
fabric, cut into 1¼"(3cm) strips,
straight corners.

Outer border: light-colored, large floral
fabric, cut into 6" (15cm) strips lengthways
down the fabric, mitered corners.

Making up the quilt and quilting

(Lessons 12 and 13)
Lay the backing, batting, and pressed front
panel one on top of the other. Quilt around
the outlines of the flowers and along the
accent border. Quilt rose and leaf patterns
over the center panel.

Binding

(Lesson 14)
Bind the basted edge with salmon pink
bias tape.

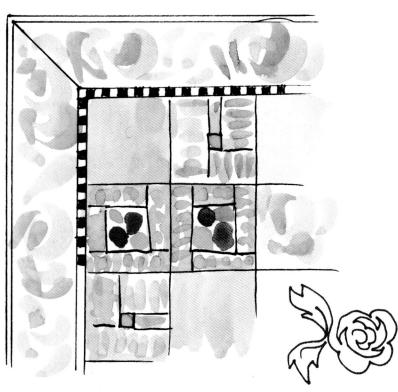

Accent border and edging design.

Quilting suggestion.

Sapphires in the Sand
87½" x 78¾" (222 x 200cm)

These sapphires, sparkling blue and turquoise between layers of earth, have been sewn onto a background created using a strip technique. Or would you prefer rubies? Emeralds? Amethysts? Pick the color of your favorite stone! The tire tracks from mining vehicles inspired the zigzag pattern of the strips.

■ Materials
Fabrics
- a total of approx. 11 yd. (10m) of as many different beige and light brown shades as possible for the layers of earth; you can add some yellow, pale pink, light green, light blue, or lilac as well
- 8" (20cm) each of 4 different plain turquoise-blue shades, gradated from light to dark, for the gemstones
- 6½ yd. (6m) light, soft cotton fabric (and/or a suitable length of thin curtain lining, sheeting, or similar) as a background fabric

Other materials
- 87" x 95" (220 x 240cm) backing fabric
- 87" x 95" (220 x 240cm) batting
- 9½ yd. (8.5m) light brown bias tape for the binding
- quilting thread in beige

Cutting guide
For each block you will need approx. 2¼ yd. (2m) of appliquéd fabric strips (1¼"–3¼" [3–8cm] in width), cut from selvage to selvage.

■ Method
70 gemstones
Cut 18 squares of approx. 4" x 4" (10 x 10cm) from each of the 4 turquoise-blue shades. Place 4 squares of different shades in a pile, right sides up. Divide the squares twice diagonally to make 4 triangles, using a ruler. Swap over the colors so that there are 4 different shades in the same order for each gemstone. The lightest should be placed opposite the darkest and the 2 medium shades should be in the same places each time.

Join up the gemstone blocks and press. Trim all the blocks to the same size; ours were exactly 2½" x 2½"(6.5 x 6.5cm).

Background fabrics
Cut 72 light background fabric pieces approx. 11¾" (30cm) square. These will form the basis of the blocks to which the

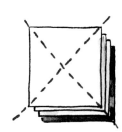

Place 4 squares of the different gemstone colors in a pile, all right sides up. Make 2 diagonal cuts to form triangles.

Assemble 4 identical gemstones each from 4 triangles.

strips are sewn. Don't use a heavy fabric (lightweight curtain lining is fine) or the quilt will become too weighty.

Cutting strips
Cut the beige and light brown fabrics into strips 1¼"–3¼" (3–8cm) wide for the layers of earth and also make a few strips 2½"(6.5cm) wide (the same width as the gemstones). These strips are joined directly to the gemstones; all the other strips can follow in any order you like. Use a ruler to cut the strips, but you don't need to be accurate to a fraction of an inch. Cut a large number of strips in a range of fabrics so you have a good selection when you are sewing.

36 x block A
Place a gemstone block on a piece of the background fabric, the lightest section facing top left, and hold in place with a pin. Now add the strips for the layers of earth. Begin with medium shades on the top right and bottom left sides of the gemstone, joining the short edges of the strip to the gemstone block, right sides together. Unfold the strips and press. Trim off the excess fabric where it overhangs the background fabric. Join a strip along both long sides, with right sides together, and unfold. Press and trim off the excess fabric at the ends.

Carry on in this manner until all the background fabric has been covered. Place the gemstones off-center to give an irregular appearance.

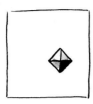

Place a gemstone on the background fabric with the lightest section top left (for block A).

Join the first strip (which is the width of the gemstone) right sides together, to the top right edge.

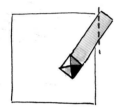

Unfold the strip, trim the excess fabric in line with the edge of the background piece.

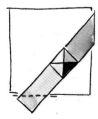

Join the second strip (also the width of the gemstone) right sides facing, to the bottom left edge of the gemstone, unfold, and trim the excess fabric in line with the edge of the background piece.

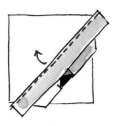

With right sides together, join the next strip to the sewn-on strips and unfold. Trim the excess fabric in line with the edge of the background piece.

Cover the entire surface of the background fabric with strips.

Block A: the lightest section of the gemstone is top left.

Block B: the lightest section of the gemstone is bottom left. When the quilt front panel is made up, this block will be turned so that the gemstone's lightest section also points to top left.

Once the square of backing fabric is completely covered with strips, press the block. Trim all the blocks to the same size; ours were exactly 10¾" x 10¾" (27 x 27cm).

Tip
You can also use the reverse of many of the fabrics to get even more earth tones.

30 x block B
The B blocks differ from the A blocks in that the gemstone is orientated with the lightest section bottom left. Join the first 2 strips to the lightest and the darkest edges of the gemstone, then continue as for block A.

6 x block C
The C blocks have no gemstone.

Tip
Sew some blocks with 2 gemstones as well; remember not to change the orientation of the gemstones (see A2 and B2 in the sewing plan).

Sewing plan

Lay out 9 rows of 8 blocks. Make "layers of earth" by alternating rows of A blocks with rows of B blocks. Insert a few blocks with 2 gemstones (A2 and/or B2) at random and alternate with a few C blocks at the border. Follow the indicated sequence of rows or make up another design if you prefer.The blocks should all be arranged so that the lightest section of the gemstone is at top left.

1st row: 7 x A, C
2nd row: C, 7 x B
3rd row: 8 x A
4th row: B, B2, 4 x B, B2, B
5th row: C, 5 x A, A2, A
6th row: 8 x B
7th row: 7 x A, C
8th row: C, 7 x B
9th row: 2 x A, A2, A, C, 3 x A

Assembly

(Lesson 10)
Join the blocks to make the quilt front panel.

Making up the quilt and quilting

(Lessons 12 and 13)
Lay the backing, batting, and pressed front panel one on top of the other. First, quilt a separate border edging 4" (10cm) in from the edges, e.g. horizontal lines running to the edge of the quilt. Fill the inner area with wide meandering lines. Don't quilt over the gemstones.

Binding

(Lesson 14)
Bind the quilt with beige-colored bias tape.

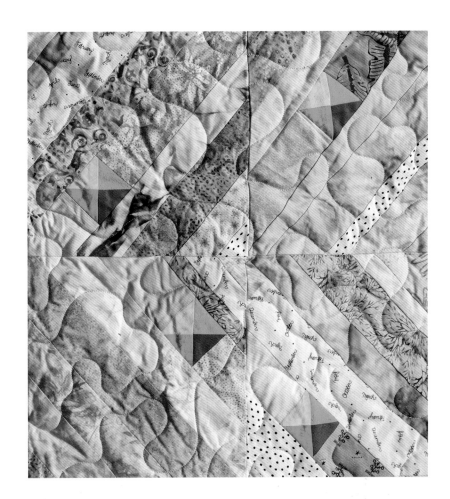

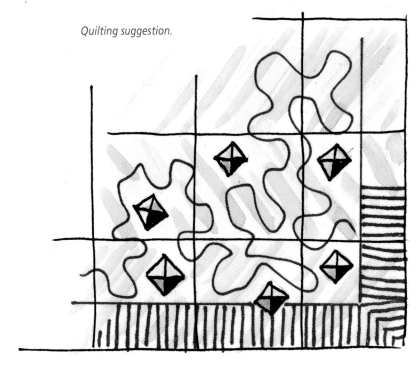

Quilting suggestion.

Vineyard Terraces
28" x 34½" (71 x 88cm)

The angled strips represent the slope of the hill, while the little huts are where the vineyard workers keep their tools. We embroidered the doors of the huts with lots of red thread but you could also create doors with red fabric.

◼ Materials
Fabrics

- 1¼ yd. (1m) approx. total length of different fall-colored fabric, in strips approx. 10" (25cm) long and ¾"–2" (2–5cm) wide, plain and lightly patterned
- 2" (5cm) each of 5–7 different shades of green, lightly patterned fabric, for the landscape
- 4" (10cm) fresh green fabric for the terrace piping and the bottom strip

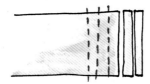

Cut strips from the short edge of the fall-colored fabrics.

- 4" (10cm) or a scrap of natural white cotton for the huts
- 4" (10cm) bright red fabric for the hut roofs and the border piping
- 20" (50cm) lilac/blue, plain or lightly patterned fabric, for the sky
- 24" (60cm) dark brown fabric for the frame

Other materials

- 32" x 39" (80 x 100cm) backing fabric
- 32" x 39" (80 x 100cm) batting
- 3¾" (3.40m) dark brown bias tape for the binding
- quilting thread in light blue, green and mid-brown

◼ Method
Vineyard terraces

Cut strips 10" (25cm) long and ¾"–2" (2–5cm) wide from as many different fall-colored fabrics as possible; you don't need to use a ruler.

Arrange the strips for the bottom terrace side by side, mixing up the colors, and offset each successive strip about ¼"–½" (½–1cm) lower than the previous strip until you have a block approx. 28" (70cm) wide (measured across the center of the block). Press all the seam allowances to the right.

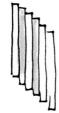

Make the bottom terrace section, joining each successive strip approx. ½" (1 cm) lower than the previous strip.

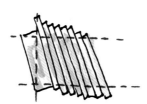

The bottom terrace section should be approx. 28" (70cm) wide (measured across the center). Trim top and bottom edges straight, and the left-hand edge so it is vertical.

To make the middle terrace, offset each strip approx. ¾" (2cm) lower than the previous strip until you have a block approx. 24" (60cm) wide (measured across the center of the block). Press all the seam allowances to the left.

For the top terrace, offset each strip approx. 1¼" (3cm) lower than the previous strip until you have a block approx. 20" (50cm) wide (measured across the center of the block). Press all the seam allowances to the right.

Add 2 wider but shorter strips to the left side of all 3 terrace blocks, so you don't lose too much fabric when you trim to size. Place each block individually onto a wide cutting mat, using the horizontal grid lines as a guide. Trim the left-hand edge vertically and then trim off the top and bottom edge horizontally. You can use 2 cutting mats for these long cuts, placing 2 rulers end-to-end. We cut the bottom terrace to 7½" (19cm), the middle to 6¾" (17cm) and the top to 4¼" (11cm) in height.

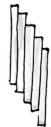

Make the middle terrace section, offsetting each successive strip by ¾"–1¼" (2–3cm).

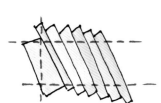

The middle terrace section should be approx. 24" (60cm) wide (measured across the center). Trim top and bottom edges straight, and the left-hand edge so it is vertical.

Join top terrace section, offsetting each successive strip by approx. 1¼"–1½" (3–4cm).

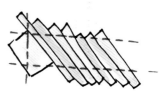

The top terrace section should be approx. 20" (50cm) wide (measured across the center). Trim top and bottom edges straight, and the left-hand edge so it is vertical.

Landscape and sky

Join several horizontal strips of green fabric to make the small bottom section of landscape. The piece should be as high as the bottom terrace section (ours was 7½" [19cm]) and approx. 6" (15cm) wide. Place the landscape section to the right of the bottom terrace section, both right sides up. Slide the landscape section under

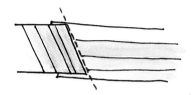

Make the first landscape section from strips of green fabric, making sure the height matches the height of the terrace section. Push the terrace over the left-hand edge of the landscape strip and cut along the edge of the vineyard. Join along this seam. Make the next section in the same manner.

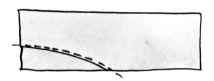

Cut a curved hill piece from green fabric and lay it onto the bottom left-hand corner of a strip of blue fabric. Cut around the shape of the hill, join the 2 pieces and tidy up the edges.

Fold 2 green piping strips (1" [2.5cm] wide). Attach the piping strips to the bottom edges of the top and middle terraces. Sew on the piping only as far as the edge of the terraces.

the terrace until the left-hand edge is completely covered, then cut along the terrace edge. Discard the unwanted piece of green fabric and join the terrace and landscape sections together. Our new section was 31½" (80cm) wide.

Repeat for the top 2 terrace sections. Our middle section was 6¾" (17cm) high and the landscape section attached to the right was made up of 3 horizontal strips of green fabric with 1 horizontal strip of blue above them. Join these strips together, then join them to the right-hand side of the terrace section as described above. The entire new section should be the same width as the bottom section.

Our top terrace section was 4¼" (11cm) high. Add a strip of blue fabric to the right-hand side of the terrace section so that the entire new section measures the same width as the bottom row. Arrange the 3 sections on your pin board.

Cut a curved hill piece from patterned green fabric. It should be 2" (5cm) high at its highest point and about 12" (30cm) long. Cut a strip of blue fabric 4¾" (12cm) high and the width of the bottom 2 sections. Place the hill, right side up, in the bottom left-hand corner of the blue strip. Cut along the curve of the hill and discard the unwanted piece of blue fabric. Join both the pieces together with a curved seam. Trim the bottom edge of the strip straight: our strip was 4" (10cm) high.

7 huts

Cut a strip exactly 2" (5cm) wide in natural white fabric and a strip 1½" (4cm) wide in red, both approx. 14" (35cm) long; join them together along their long edges. Press the seam allowance toward the white side. Cut 5 sections from the strip you have just made, each exactly 2½" (6cm) wide. Fold in the sides to make a seam allowance and fold down the top corners to make a pointed roof shape in the red fabric. Press the pieces. Fix the folded edges with pins and arrange the huts on the vineyard so that their bottom edges can be slipped into the horizontal seams. Push the huts on the top layer deeper into the seam or fold the huts to make them smaller.

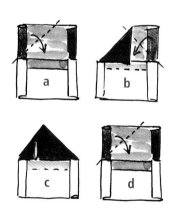

Fold the huts as shown (a to d) and hold in place with pins.

Sewing plan

Join a 2" (5cm)-wide strip of green fabric to the bottom edge of the lowest terrace piece, sliding 2 huts into the seam. Cut 2 strips of mid-green fabric 1" (2.5cm) wide and approx. 28" (70cm) long. Fold in half lengthways, wrong sides facing and press flat. Join a strip of green piping to the lower edges of the middle and top terraces, making sure it reaches the end of each terrace. The ends will eventually be covered by a hut.

Join up the terrace sections, sliding the bottom edges of the huts into the seams. At the right-hand edge of each terrace insert a hut to hide the end of the green piping. Press the seam allowances toward the bottom, but press the piping toward the top.

Fold the huts upward and appliqué them by hand or with the machine using thread of a suitable color. I used red thread to sew on the huts and at the same time created red doors with freehand embroidered lines. Press the finished panel and trim the outer edges so that they are straight and at right angles.

Adding a border
(Lesson 11)
Piping: red fabric, cut into ¾" (2cm) strips, straight corners.
Outer border: dark brown fabric, cut into 4¾" (12cm) strips, mitered corners.

Making up the quilt and quilting
(Lessons 12 and 13)
Lay the backing, batting, and the pressed front panel one on top of the other. Quilt a dense pattern (stippling) in the sky and slanted, slightly curved lines across the terrace strips, with wavy horizontal lines across the green landscape and straight lines running across the outer border.

Binding
(Lesson 14)
Bind the basted quilt edge with dark brown bias tape.

Finishing
Make a hanger casing to the back of the top edge.

Join up the sections. Add a strip of green fabric at the base.

Tuck the huts into the seams, fold up, and sew on—we used red thread. Create a door with the same thread by machine stitching up and down in close lines.

Canyon Colors
95½" x 86½" (243 x 220cm)

The aim here was to reproduce the interplay between the vibrant colors in the different rock strata in the canyons of Arizona using a technique with strips of fabric. The quilt front panel is heavily quilted.

◼ Materials
Fabrics
- 10" (25cm) each of 14 or more deep shades, e.g. purple, deep violet, maroon (color group A)
- 10" (25cm) each of 13 or more warm shades, e.g. scarlet, orange, magenta (color group B)
- 10" (25cm) each of 20 or more medium shades, e.g. lilac, mauve, pink (color group C)
- 10" (25cm) each of 8 or more light shades, e.g. apricot, salmon, pale pink (color group D)
- To make the strips sections, buy long quarters or fat quarters of plain, hand-dyed fabrics, batiks, or lightly patterned fabrics. Scraps of fabric of a suitable length (approx. 22" [55cm]) will increase the range of colors.
- 2¼ yd. (2m) yellow fabric for the piping around the light sections
- 1¼ yd. (1m) green fabric for the piping around the dark sections

Other materials
- 103" x 95" (260 x 240cm) backing fabric
- 103" x 95" (260 x 240cm) batting
- 10½ yd. (9.50cm) bias tape in purple or maroon for the binding
- quilting thread in pale pink, lilac, red, and purple

Cutting guide
- 10" (25cm) fabric is enough for 1 strip section (approx. 20" x 12" [50 x 30cm]).

◼ Method
Strip sections
(Lesson 5: Working with strips)
Sort your fabrics into 4 color groups A, B, C, and D. Divide the long quarters lengthways into pieces approx. 22" (55cm) long. Press the fabrics.

Cut the first color group into strips of approx. 1¼"–2¾" (3–7cm) wide. Cut the strips without using a ruler so they are irregular; this will make the sections look more vibrant. Mix up the strip colors well. Join the strips of fabric along their long edges to make sections at least 12" (30cm) in height. Begin and end with a slightly wider strip. Alternate the colors so that no two identical colors are adjacent. First, press the sections from the wrong side to lay all the seam allowances in the same direction, then press from the right side to smooth the fabric, slightly pulling the strips away from one another.

You will need:
Deep purple group A:	14 sections
Warm red group B:	13 sections
Medium lilac group C:	20 sections
Light apricot group D:	8 sections

Trim all the sections along their long edges to exactly 11¾" (30cm) high, leaving the short ends untrimmed.

A

B

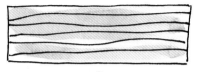

C

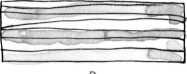

D

Sort the fabrics into color groups A to D and cut strips of half the fabric width. Make sections in each color group, press and trim to a height of exactly 11¾" (30cm).

Sewing plan

You need to make 9 rows approx. 90½" (230cm) wide. Make the color sections within each row irregular, with waves, angles, or curves, marking the borders of the colors with a piped edge, then join the piped edge onto the adjacent strip section. Trim the fabric pieces behind the piped edge to approx. ½" (1cm) seam allowance. If any area in the same color group has to be wider than 20" (50cm), join 2 sections together with no piped edge and a wavy or straight (but angled) seam.

Be sure to pay attention to the way the colors match up between the sections as you work.

Trim the long edges of the sections so they are straight. The rows don't have to be all equal in size, but there shouldn't be any crooked edges. Join the 9 rows together and don't worry if the color borders don't meet exactly. Trim the outer edges of the quilt to size.

Tip

Arrange the rows along the horizontal guide lines of your cutting mat to ensure they are straight. Hold the hemmed piping in place with pins before sewing.

Tip

Use an aluminum flat bar from the DIY store as a ruler when cutting the long edges.

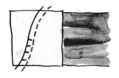

Piped edge: lay piping fabric on top of the strip section (ours were red), draw the curved line, and sew along it. Trim off outside the line (the black line on the left) leaving a seam allowance. Clip the seam allowance.

Fold the piping fabric behind the strip section and push flat, leaving 1/16" (1–2mm) showing. Press.

Lay the shaped edge onto the adjacent strip section and join (shown here on the red strip section). Trim away the excess fabric at the back.

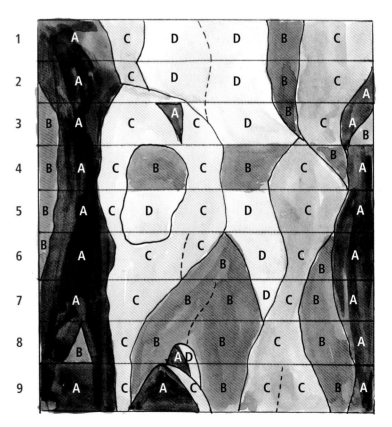

Sewing plan: work in rows. Make the color sections irregular shapes and mark them with piped edges in yellow or green. You may need to join sections of similar color to make wider areas; don't pipe these (shown as dashes here). Make 9 rows.

2 rocks

Make the 2 rocks for the bottom of the quilt as piped appliqué motifs (Lesson 8). First, join a light and a dark strip section together with a curved seam (see diagram). Press and trim the seam allowance. With right sides facing, place the two-color piece onto a piece of yellow piping fabric and draw the rock shape onto the piping fabric (so the shape will not be reversed when finished). Sew along the line and cut out, leaving a seam allowance. Clip the seam allowance and turn right side out. Push the piping out a little and press. Make the second rock in the same

manner. The small rock at the back should be made from color groups A and D and is approx. 9" (22cm) wide and 11" (28cm) high. It should be slightly taller than the large rock. The large rock should be made from color groups A and C and be approx. 19" (49cm) wide and 10" (25cm) high. It should cover the bottom edge of the small rock and should be placed on the bottom edge of the quilt. Attach the rocks along their piped edges. Trim the excess piping fabric and the quilt front behind the appliqué motifs.

Large geographical feature

The quilt is made more interesting with a large, irregular "opening" that in this case hasn't been formed by wind and water but was created using piping techniques (see Lesson 8). Place a square of yellow fabric approx. 31½" x 31½" (80 x 80cm) onto the quilt, right sides facing. Using sweeping strokes, draw an irregular ellipse or circular shape onto the yellow fabric. The outline we made was approx. 17" (43cm) wide and approx. 24" (60cm) high.

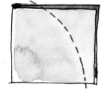

To make the rocks, place a section A and a section D together, both right sides up, and make a curved cut as shown for the shadow line on the rock.

With right sides facing, place the piping fabric and the two-color piece together, draw a rock shape, and sew along the line. Cut around the line, clip the seam allowance, and turn the stone right side out. Press.

Swap over the colors, joining the light right-hand piece to the dark left-hand piece with a curved seam.

Overlap the stones and sew them onto the front of the quilt, trimming off the excess fabric at the back. The bottom rock sits on the bottom edge of the quilt.

To make the large opening, lay the piping fabric, right sides facing, onto the front of the quilt. Draw the outline of the opening. Sew along the line and cut out the opening, leaving a seam allowance. Clip the seam allowance and push the piping fabric through the opening to the back. Pin the piping in place. Place a background piece that you have made behind the opening and join it on. Trim the excess fabric from the back of the quilt.

Tip
You will easily be able to feel the piping seams under the yellow piping fabric, which will make it easy to draw the "opening" in the correct position.

Sew along the line you have drawn. Cut both layers of fabric (the piping fabric and the quilt front) inside the line you have sewn, leaving a seam allowance. Clip the seam allowance at approx. ½" (1cm) intervals. Fold the yellow fabric through the opening and

pin the edge in place. About ¹⁄₁₆" (1–2mm) of the yellow piped edge should be visible.

Join a red and a light strip section together. Pin this piece behind the opening with the red section at the top. Stitch it on with an unobtrusive color thread, sewing around the opening. Trim the excess fabric from the back of the quilt (the yellow fabric and the quilt front strip section).

Making up the quilt and quilting
(Lessons 12 and 13)
Lay the backing, batting, and pressed

front panel one on top of the other. Quilt irregular, gentle wavy lines onto all the colored sections and fill the spaces in between the lines with a border pattern. If you are longarm machine quilting, give each section its own border pattern, matching the thread to the fabric color. If you are hand quilting, stitch along the strips and the piping seams.

Binding
(Lesson 14)
Bind the basted quilt edge with purple bias tape.

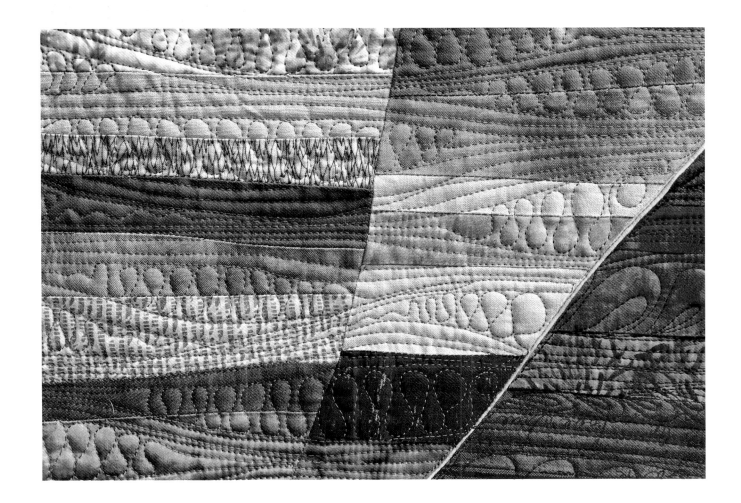

Gecko Pillow
19½" x 19½" (50 x 50cm)

This a great practice project for freehand machine quilting, whether you are using a household sewing machine or a longarm quilting machine. Give free rein to your imagination and use all kinds of patterns to decorate the gecko's body as he scurries across the rock.

■ Materials
Fabrics

- 12" (30cm) black or very dark brown fabric for the center
- 10" (25cm) sand or orange, plain or lightly patterned fabric for the background
- 2" (5cm) beige-and-white striped fabric or cream fabric for the piping (or whatever you prefer)
- 12" (30cm) brown-red-purple striped fabric for the border

Other materials

- 24" x 24" (60 x 60cm) lining fabric
- 24" x 24" (60 x 60cm) batting
- 24" x 28" (60 x 70cm) backing fabric of an appropriate color
- variegated quilting thread in shades of yellow-purple-brown
- gecko quilting template (of your choice)
- white chalk marker pencil
- 16"–18" (40–45cm) zipper

■ Method
Pillow front panel

(Lesson 6: Curved seams)
Cut a square approx. 12" x 12" (30 x 30cm) from the darkest fabric and cut a flattened S-shaped curve along all 4 edges. Cut 2 squares of approx. 10" x 10" (25 x 25cm) from the sand-colored fabric and divide each in half diagonally.

Cut the edges of the central square (approx. 12" x 12" [30 x 30cm]) with a flattened S-shape curve.

Trim off the excess corners of the first triangle. Cut the second triangle in the same way and join up.

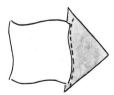

Place one edge of the center section along the long edge of an outer triangle (made from approx. 10" x 10" [25 x 25cm] squares cut in half diagonally) and cut along the curved edge.

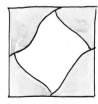

When all 4 triangles are attached, cut the piece to an exact square.

Lay one of the curved edges of the center section along the diagonal of a triangle, both fabrics right sides up. Overlap the edge of the center section slightly and cut the fabric of the triangle along the curve, using the shape of the center section as a template. Trim the overhanging corners of the triangle in line with the edges of the center section. Join with a curved seam. Do the same with the opposite edge and then both the remaining edges. Press the seam allowances to the outside. Cut the completed piece to make an exact square; ours was 15" x 15" (38 x 38cm).

Piping strip
(Lesson 8)
Cut a strip exactly ¾" (2cm) wide from beige-and-white striped or cream colored fabric, fold it in half lengthways, and sew it on around the edges.

Adding the border
(Lesson 11)
Sew a strip of striped fabric of a suitable color around the center section, ours was 4" (10cm) wide. Make mitered corners.

Add a piping strip and border, then assemble the layers and quilt.

Tip
There are plenty of pictures of geckos to be found on the internet (do an image search); pick one to work from where the entire creature is shown from above. Print the image, trace the outline, and enlarge it to the size you want. Make a cardboard template or, if you have the skills, draw the animal freehand.

Making up the quilt and quilting
(Lessons 12 and 13)
Lay the pillow lining, batting, and front panel one on top of the other. Quilt straight lines radiating outward across the striped border and a curved decorative border across the long edges of the triangles. You might like to copy the design on page 102. The gecko on our pillow measured 9" (23cm) from head to the tip of its tail. Trace the outline of the gecko onto the dark central panel using a white chalk pencil. Draw in the line of its back, then use the sewing machine to quilt the outline of the gecko and its spine as a double line of stitches before adding the details. I emphasized the joints with spiral patterns, created a row of small circles along the back, and divided the body into small areas filled with wavy lines, zigzags, and ellipse shapes. I left the eyes as an outline. Finally, sew along all the main lines another five or six times to emphasize the shape.

Adding a zipper
(Lesson 15)
Make the back of the pillow, inserting a zipper, and attach to the pillow front.

Quilting suggestion for the Gecko.

Wintry Night
69" x 63" (175 x 160cm)

The use of white and gray here is elegant and atmospheric. The stars in the night sky shine down onto the landscape below, built up in layers of decreasing size from foreground to horizon, creating depth and distance.

■ Materials
Fabrics

- 2 yd. (1.80m) fabric shaded from light gray to black, delicately patterned, for the sky and the binding
- 10" (25cm) each of 2 different light gray fabrics, plain or patterned
- 20" (50cm) each of 3 different shades of white and ecru for the landscape
- 1¼ yd. (1m) pure white for the foreground
- 6" (15cm) strips of fabric in light gray or gray with white and/or ecru for the fence rows
- 4" (10cm) woven check pattern, dark on unbleached white cotton, for the fence rows
- 1¼ yd. (1m) each of white and unbleached white cotton for the snowflakes (or 150 white and 150 unbleached white cotton circles, 3¼" [8cm] in diameter).

Other materials
- 75" x 71" (190 x 180cm) backing fabric
- 75" x 71" (190 x 180cm) batting
- quilting thread in light gray and white

■ Method
Landscape
(Lesson 6: Curved seams)

Cut a strip approx. 20" (50cm) wide from the dark part of the shaded fabric and set it aside for the binding. Pin the lighter piece of the fabric to the pin board with the lightest part at the bottom. Arrange the light-colored landscape fabrics beneath it in the order you want. Spread out the landscape fabrics over at least 71"(180cm) if necessary, so they cover the entire width of the quilt front.

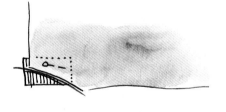

Working from top to bottom, place the shaded sky fabric (darker area at the top) on a sufficiently large work surface. Cut the bottom edge at a slight angle to make a natural curved shape. Place the next layer of fabric on the work surface, overlapping it with the bottom edge of the sky fabric. Hold the layers of fabric together with a few pins. Using scissors, cut the bottom fabric along the line of the upper sky layer. Remove the pins and discard the excess scrap of fabric. The cut edges of both fabrics will now match. Insert marker pins about a handbreadth apart in both the top and bottom fabrics; these will help when you are joining up the seam.

Cut the top fabric edge to shape. Slide the next layer of fabric (here a striped fabric) underneath and hold it in place with pins. Cut the bottom fabric along the edge of the upper fabric. Remove the excess scrap from underneath the fabric. Join both fabrics together. Trim to shape again, if necessary.

Slide the next layer of fabric under the piece you have just made. Cut along the new lower edge and remove the scrap beneath the fabric. Join the fabrics together.

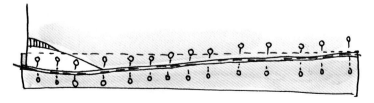

Place some marker pins at opposite sides at intervals of about a handbreadth. The pairs of pins should match up as you are joining the seam.

Use the free arm of your sewing machine if possible. Place the fabrics, right sides facing, with the larger piece of fabric underneath. Sew from top to bottom, letting the top fabric run loosely through your left hand and the bottom fabric run loosely through your right and placing the edges of the fabric together as you sew. Make sure that the pairs of marker pins stay level. If the edges get out of alignment, you may have to pull the top and/or the bottom fabric a little to ensure you get a seam with no lumps or folds.

Sewing plan

If you want to make an exact copy of the suggested quilt, please refer to the diagram and the photo; the numbers refer to the order of sewing.

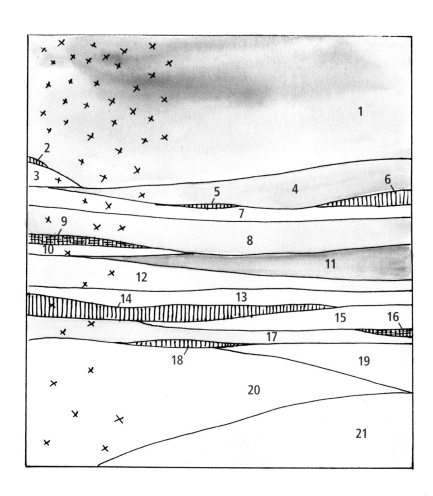

1 = fabric shaded from light to dark gray
2 = striped fabric on the hill to the left
3 = ecru fabric for the hill to the left
4 = light, warm gray fabric running the full width of the quilt and tapering away to the left
5 = striped fabric, small area in the center below fabric 4
6 = striped fabric, to the right below fabric 4
7 = pure white, running the full width of the quilt
8 = warm light gray, running the full width of the quilt, a little higher in the middle than at the sides
9 = checkered pattern, half the width of the quilt, tapering from the left to the center
10 = pure white, below the checkered pattern fabric, reaching a little farther toward the center
11 = cool gray, running the full width of the quilt, tapering away to the left
12 = creamy white, running the full width of the quilt, wider on the left than the right

13 = pure white, running the full width of the quilt
14 = striped fabric, two-thirds of the width of the quilt, tapering to the right
15 = light ecru, half the width of the quilt, tapering from the right to the center
16 = checkered pattern, small area tapering to the left
17 = ecru, running the full width of the quilt
18 = striped fabric, small area in the center, below fabric 17
19 = off-white, deep area, half the width of the quilt, tapering up toward the center
20 = pure white, large area reaching the bottom edge of the quilt, running the full width of the quilt, tapering to a point to the right
21 = light ecru, large area reaching the bottom edge of the quilt, tapering to a point to the left

Making up the quilt and quilting
(Lessons 12 and 13)

Lay the backing, batting, and front panel one on top of the other and quilt. Using the machine, work layers of texture to represent air currents and eddies in the sky and create lots of different diagonal border patterns on the snowfields. If you are quilting by hand, I suggest simple lines to represent air currents in the sky and gently curving diagonal lines for the snowfields.

Binding
(Lesson 14)

Bind the basted quilt edge with a straight-cut strip of dark gray fabric 2½" (6cm)-wide, cut from the strip of shaded sky fabric you set aside.

300 snowflakes

Cut 150 unbleached cotton and 150 pure white fabric circles; ours were 2¾" (7cm) across, but 3¼" (8cm) would have been better. Make 300 yo-yos. Use a handy commercial "yo-yo maker" (for 3¼" [8cm] circles) if you have one, or make the yo-yos in the conventional manner: fold a narrow hem around the fabric circles, approx. ⅛" (3 mm), and make a row of running stitches around the edge through both layers of fabric. Pull on the thread to gather the yo–yo. Flatten the yo-yo and secure the thread with a few stitches, leaving approx. 8" (20cm) of thread to attach the yo-yo. Arrange the yo-yos at random over the entire quilt and hold in place with pins. The yo-yos at the top should be more densely packed than those at the bottom. Attach each yo-yo to the quilt using the long trailing thread, making small stitches at 4 opposing points or sewing in the center like a button.

Finishing

Make a hanger casing at the back of the top edge.

Fold a narrow hem in a fabric circle. Sew a running stitch around the hem with quilting thread. Leave a long trailing thread.

Pull on the thread and gather the fabric tightly to form a pouch.

Flatten the yo-yo and secure the thread with a few stitches.

Attach the yo–yo using the long trailing thread, fixing it in place either at 4 opposing points or in the center like a button.

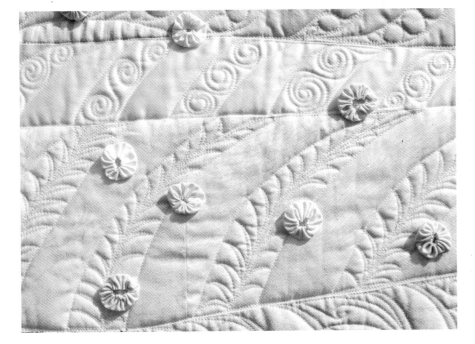

Ancient Pyramids
19½" x 23½" (50 x 60cm)

Although these pyramids are not made using a freehand cutting technique, you don't need to use templates. Scraps of fabric are all you need for the pyramids, while quilted strips form the frame.

■ Materials
Fabrics
- scraps of fabric approx. 3½" x 6" (8 x 15cm) in 3 different light shades for the pyramid sides in the sun
- scraps of fabric approx. 6" x 6" (15 x 15cm) in 3 different dark shades for the sides in shadow
- 4" (10cm) sand-colored fabric for the foreground
- 10" (25cm) mid-blue fabric for the sky
- 4" (10cm) ecru fabric for the inner border
- 12" (30cm) dark, woven, striped fabric for the outer border

Other materials
- 22" x 26" (55 x 65cm) backing fabric
- 22" x 26" (55 x 65cm) batting
- quilting thread in blue, yellow, dark red, ecru
- square ruler (8" x 8" [20 x 20cm] or larger)
- picture frame with removable glass 20" x 24" (50 x 60cm)

■ Method
Assembling the pyramid sides
Cut strips approx. 6" (15cm) long and 3½" (8cm) wide from the light fabrics scraps and squares of approx. 6" (15cm) from the dark fabrics. Arrange them by shade. Pyramid 1 is the darkest, pyramid 2 is in medium shades, and pyramid 3 is the lightest; this applies to the sides in both the sun and in shadow. Join a light strip to the appropriate dark square in each case, pressing each seam flat.

3 pyramids
Place the fabric pieces horizontally on the cutting mat, with the light fabric to the left. Place the square ruler on the fabric so that the left-hand edge is at an angle of 30° to the vertical seam, with the end of the seam at the corner of the ruler. Cut the top edges of the pyramid at a right angle. Arrange the pyramids as shown: pyramid 3, the smallest, is on the right. Pyramid 2, the biggest, overlaps it, the baseline aligned with pyramid 3. Pyramid 1 is the top layer with its baseline approx. 1¼" (3cm) lower. Cut the bases in a straight line so that the pyramids are the correct height.

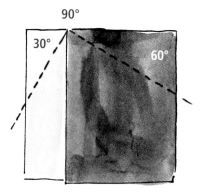

Join up the light and dark fabrics and place the corner of the ruler on the top edge aligned with the seam. The ruler should lie at an angle of about 30° to the vertical seam. Cut the top corners along the edges of the ruler.

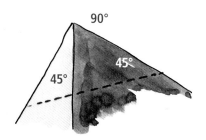

Cut the bases of the pyramids straight. The 2 base angles of the pyramid are 45° each.

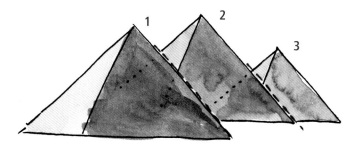

Lay out pyramids 1, 2, and 3 to overlap; trim the left edges of pyramids 2 and 3 along the overlapping edges.

Assembling the picture

Trim the left-hand edges of pyramids 2 and 3 where they overlap. Remove the bottom left-hand corner of pyramid 1 at an angle of 45°. The cut should start at the bottom seam of the pyramid. Join an approx. 8" (20cm)-long blue strip to the lighter side of each pyramid that is the same width as the left-hand edge of the pyramid. Press the seam allowance toward the blue fabric side. Trim the right-hand fabric edges by approx. ¼" (0.5cm) so that the tip of the pyramid won't be lost in the seams that follow. Cut the left-hand bottom corner from a 6" (15cm)-wide and approx. 16" (40cm)-long blue strip at an angle of 45° and set it aside. Join the blue strip to the right-hand edge of pyramid 3. The bottom edges of pyramid 3 and the blue strip of sky should align.

Join pyramid 3 to pyramid 2. Trim the top edge of the picture straight (level with the shortest piece of fabric) and cut the right-hand edge vertical. This will leave approx. 2" (5cm) of blue fabric to the right and approx. 1½" (4cm) of blue above pyramid 2.

Divide the sand-colored fabric down the center to make 2 strips, 4" (10cm) in length. Cut a 1½" (4cm)-wide strip from one of these pieces and join it to the bottom edge of the section with pyramids 2 and 3.

Arrange pyramid 1 with the two other pyramids, the bottom edge in line with the bottom edge of the sand-colored strip. The distance to pyramid 2 should be approx. 3¼" (8cm) (measured at an angle). Join pyramid 1 to the left-hand edge of the 2-pyramid section, pressing all the seams after sewing.

Take the blue corner you set aside and place it at the left-hand edge of the pyramids, checking that the orientation is correct. Join the remaining 1½" (4cm)-wide sand-colored strip to the bottom edge. Trim the right-hand edge of the sand-colored strip to form a right-angled triangle. Place the two-piece triangle on the right-hand diagonal edge, making sure that the sky and pyramid meet the seam of the sand-colored strip exactly. Hold in place with pins and check again before sewing. Add an approx. 4" (10cm)-deep sand-colored strip across the bottom of the entire piece. Press the panel and trim the edges to an exact rectangle; ours was 16½" x 10¾" (42 x 27cm).

Using a long, straight stitch, carefully sew around the blue edges within the seam allowances to secure the diagonally cut edges.

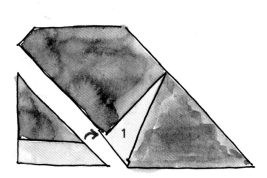

Join a blue strip to the left–hand edge of pyramid 1; it should be as wide as the pyramid edge and approx. 8" (20cm) long. Cut off the bottom left-hand corner of pyramid 1 at an angle of 45°. The cut should start at the bottom seam of the pyramid. Join a 1½" (4cm)–high sand-colored strip to the bottom edge of a triangle of blue fabric. Trim to make a right-angled triangle. Join to pyramid 1 so that the left–hand corner of the pyramid and the seam of the sand–colored strip meet exactly.

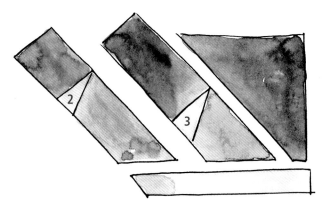

Join a blue strip to pyramid 2 and to pyramid 3; each strip should be approx. 8" (20cm) long and as wide as the left-hand edge of the pyramid. Join a blue triangle to the right-hand edge of pyramid 3 and join up pyramids 2 and 3, attaching an approx. 1½" (4cm)-deep sand-colored strip along the bottom. Neaten the edges.

Adding a border
(Lesson 11)

Inner border: cut a strip of ecru fabric
1" (2.5cm) wide.

Outer border: cut a strip of dark, woven,
striped fabric 4" (10cm) wide.

Join both strips together along their long
edges, and then make mitered corners.

Making up the quilt and quilting
(Lessons 12 and 13)

Lay the backing, batting, and pressed
front panel one on top of the other. Quilt
closely-spaced vertical lines on the sky
and closely-spaced horizontal lines on
the sand, leaving the pyramids unquilted.
Quilt light ecru lines along the seam
between the inner and outer borders.
The outer border should also have some
radiating lines in dark red.

Finishing

Place the glass of the frame on the quilt
and trim off the edges all around. Attach
your textile picture with narrow strips of
double-sided tape as close to the edge
of the back of the frame as possible.
You don't need to use the glass.

*Add a sand-colored strip across the bottom edge of the panel. Trim the panel
to an exact rectangle. Add the borders and quilt closely spaced parallel lines.*

LINES

Lesson 7:
Twigs and Branches

Projects: Four seasons: spring, summer, fall, and winter; Wintry night; Colors of the fall

Cutting out

Cut a square no smaller than 4" x 4" (10 x 10cm), but no larger than 10" x 10" (25 x 25cm). You'll be working with rectangles in the "Colors of the Fall" quilt. Get the color, size, and number from the project instructions. To make the branches, you will need fabric strips approx. ¾" (2cm) wide and as long as possible.

> **Tip**
> For a large block of 8" x 8" (20 x 20cm), cut 2 strips, each ¾" (2cm) wide from selvage to selvage for the twigs and branches.

Cutting twigs and branches

Place a square of tree fabric in front of you on the cutting mat. Divide the square diagonally from corner to corner and slide the two pieces a little apart. Cut a few side branches radiating outward from the diagonal. Slide the pieces apart without changing their position. Now cut further divisions into the pieces for the short twigs. Again, slide all the pieces apart without changing their position.

> **Tip**
> To keep the pieces in the right position while you are working, identify the outer edge of each piece of fabric with a small pencil mark (shown in red in the illustration).

Divide the square in half diagonally. Slide the pieces apart.

Make cuts for the branches that radiate from the diagonal.

Make cuts for the twigs that radiate from the branches. Indicate the outer edge of each part with a small mark.

First, insert the twigs, pressing the seam allowances toward the outside and trimming off the excess fabric in line with the outer edges.

Insert the branches, pressing the seam allowances toward the outside and trimming off the excess in line with the outer edges.

Join to the other half, before inserting the main diagonal trunk. Trim to an exact square.

Make blocks of different sizes.

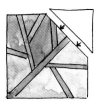

Trim off a corner of the block and replace with a triangle of background fabric, if the instructions require it.

Inserting the short branches

Start with the short twigs that you cut last, inserting darker strips of fabric into the gaps. Let the strips overhang about ½–¾" (1–2cm) at the ends. Run your fingernail down each seam or press the seam allowances immediately after sewing. Press the seam allowances toward the tree fabric side. Now trim the excess ends of the strips level with the outer edges of the section. Pay attention to the positioning of the pieces and make sure you don't get any the wrong way round.

Inserting the longer branches

Place the finished pieces on the cutting mat beside the sewing machine, making sure they are the right way round. Once all the short strips are inserted, add in the longer strips as branches.

Assembling a block

Make the second half of the block in the same way. Steam press both halves. Trim the long diagonal edges straight, using a ruler. Sew a strip into the diagonal of the block to make the trunk and press the seam allowances toward the inset strip. Press the whole block once more and trim it to the size required (see project).

Dividing a rectangle

For the "Colors of the Fall" quilt, you will be working with rectangles as your basic shape. Place the rectangle lengthways on the cutting mat. Cut the 4 corners as close to a right angle as possible and set aside. Divide the block lengthways down the center.

Cut off the 4 corners of a rectangle at an angle of 45° and set aside. Make the cuts for the trunk and branches.

Inserting the branches and trunk

Make three to four straight cuts on the right- and left-hand sides, angled upward. Insert the branches, as described above. Press the seam allowances of the branches outward. Trim the center edges and insert the trunk. Press the seam allowances toward the trunk side. Carry on making the pieces as described in the project.

Insert the branches, trimming the edges, before finally inserting the trunk.

Lesson 7

Lesson 8:
Piping Techniques

Our piping technique is a variation of reverse appliqué, also known as "mola," and is done with the sewing machine. You will need fabric for the block and/or the appliqué motif, a piping fabric of a contrasting color, and a fabric that will lie behind it. This technique is suitable for open or closed shapes and also for appliqué motifs.

Piping an opening or doorway
Projects: Desert dwellings, Canyon colors

Place the piping fabric on the block fabric, right sides facing. Draw the edge shape you want (e.g. arch, doorway, etc.) onto the piping fabric and sew along the line you have drawn. Cut both fabrics, leaving a seam allowance beyond the line.

Clip the seam allowances at intervals of ¼"–½" (0.5–1cm) up to the seam, but without cutting the thread of the seam. Pull the piping fabric through the opening to the wrong side and run your fingernail along the edge. It looks best when about ¹⁄₁₆" (1–2mm) of the piping fabric is visible. Press.

Place the fabric for the shape (e.g. white for an arch) behind the opening, pin it in place, and stitch along the edges from the front around the opening. Use an unobtrusive thread the same color as the quilt front and don't stitch into the piped edge. Finally, trim away the excess edges of the piping and the backing fabric on the wrong side.

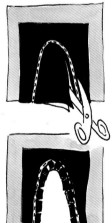

Lay the piping fabric onto the quilt block, right sides facing, with the bottom edges aligned. Draw an arc, sew along the line, and cut both layers of fabric inside the line.

Clip the seam allowance and pull the piping fabric through the opening to the back. Flatten the piping edge and press.

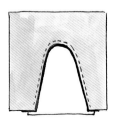

Place a different colored piece of fabric behind the opening and stitch around the edge. Trim off any excess fabric from the back.

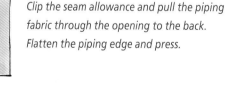

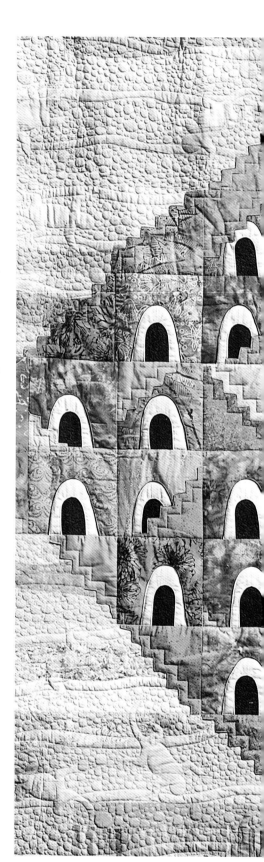

Lesson 8

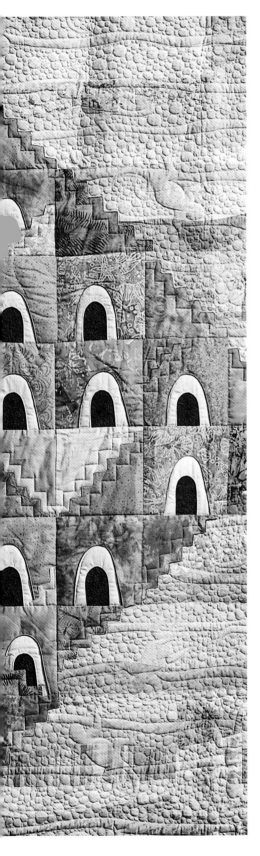

Shaping piped edges

Projects: Desert dwellings, Canyon colors, Meandering river

Piping techniques can also be used to sew unusual shaped edges. Place the piping fabric on top of the edge of the piece of fabric you are working on, right sides facing, and draw the desired shape onto the piping fabric. Sew a line of stitching about the width of the sewing machine foot in from the line. Trim off the excess fabric along the line.

Clip the seam allowance close to the seam. Fold the piping fabric to the back to reveal the right side of the fabric. Flatten the edge, leaving approx. ⅛" (1–2mm) of the piping fabric visible. Press. Place the piped edge on top of the adjacent piece of fabric, both right sides up. Pin the edge and stitch along the edge of the piping using a matching thread. Trim off any excess fabric from the back of the piece, leaving a seam allowance.

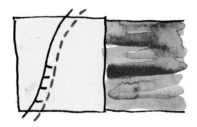

Lay the piping fabric onto the first fabric (shown in red here), draw the line you want and sew a line of stitching parallel to it. Cut off fabric a seam allowance away from the line (ours was on the left) and clip the seam allowance.

Fold the piping fabric around the edge to the back and flatten, allowing ⅟₁₆" (1–2mm) of the piping to be visible. Press.

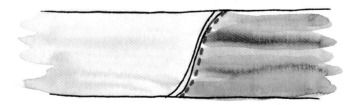

Lay the shaped edge onto the adjacent piece of fabric, both right sides up, and join (stitching onto the red section shown here). Trim off the excess fabric at the back of the piece.

Lesson 8

Hemmed appliqué with a piped edge
Projects: Canyon colors, Quarry face

Hemmed appliqué motifs can also look good with contrasting piped edges. Lay the appliqué fabric on the work surface and place the piping fabric on top, right sides facing. Trace the shape the right way round onto the piping fabric.

Sew around the outline, leaving either one side open or sewing around all the sides. Cut the shape out around the line you have sewn, leaving a seam allowance all round. Clip the seam allowance at ¼" (0.5cm) intervals. Trim the corners right up to the stitching line.

Turn the shape to the right side through the gap you have left or cut a slit approx. 2" (5cm) long in the piping fabric and turn the shape to the right side through this. Flatten the edges. Decide at which edge you want the piping fabric to be visible

(it can only be one side) and push the piping out ¹⁄₁₆" (1–2mm) to that side. Appliqué the shape onto the quilt using a matching color thread.

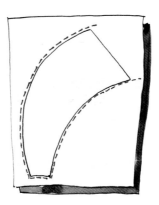

Place the appliqué fabric and piping fabric together, right sides facing. Draw the motif shape onto the piping fabric. Sew around the edges of the shape, leaving a short edge to turn right side out. Cut around the shape and clip the seam allowance up to the seam, clipping off the corners or cutting into the angle if necessary. Turn the appliqué motif right side out through the opening. Press and make the piped edge visible on your chosen side.

Place the appliqué fabric and piping fabric together, right sides facing, and draw the shape. Sew all round the shape.

Cut out the shape and clip the seam allowances (cutting corners at an angle if required). Carefully cut a slit approx. 2" (5cm) long in the piping fabric.

Turn the shape right side out through the slit, and make sure the piping fabric is visible on the side you have chosen. Appliqué the shape by hand or with the machine, using edge stitching and a matching thread.

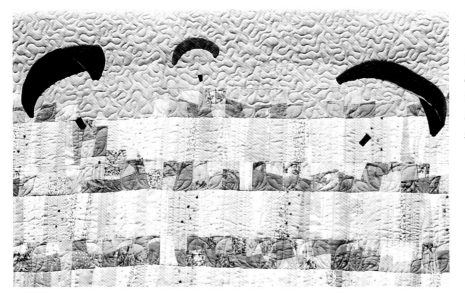

Lesson 9:
Accent Strips
Projects: Spruce plantation, Wintry night, Desert dwellings

Accent strips are a geometrical element of a design and should be made to exact measurements. They are therefore cut to size with a ruler and sewn with a scant ¼" (0.5cm) seam. Use 2 fabrics with strongly contrasting colors, such as black and white, orange and blue, light green and pink, etc.

Cut several strips of equal size from the contrasting fabrics, e.g. 2 strips, each 2" (5cm) wide, from white and black fabric. Use the ruler for this. Join the strips in alternate colors along their long edges. Divide these sections into quarters and join them along their long edges as before, always pressing the seam allowances toward the dark fabric side.

Tip
Don't make these sections wider than 24" (60cm) or you won't be able to use your quilting ruler.

From the section you have just made, cut several sections the same width as the first strip of fabric. Join these to make a ribbon that is long enough for the area that you wish to edge.

Tip
If you are really in a hurry, you can use a preprinted, striped fabric as an accent strip.

Cut strips and join them along their long edges.
Cut sections the same width as the strip of fabric.

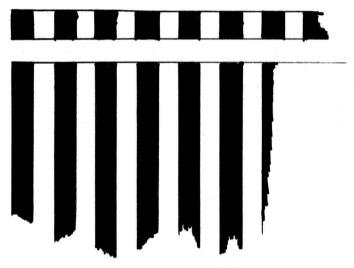

Join up the sections to make a long piece of fabric.

Four Seasons: Winter
35½" x 19½" (90 x 50cm)

Quilt this tree in its spring, summer, fall, and winter forms to make a decorative hanging for each season. Change them as the year progresses, or display all four together.

■ Materials
Fabrics
- 24" (60cm) dark-gray spotted fabric for the trunk, branches, and binding
- 24" (60cm) plain white for the snow
- 32" (80cm) unbleached cotton fabric for the background and the border

Other materials
- 24" (60cm) broderie anglaise lace (e.g. pillow edging), approx. 4" (10cm) wide, for the snow on the ground
- 39" x 24" (100 x 60cm) backing fabric
- 39" x 24" (100 x 60cm) batting
- quilting thread in white, ecru, and black
- soft pencil

■ Method
Preparation
Cut 3 strips exactly 2½" (6cm) wide from the dark gray fabric and set aside for the binding. Cut another 3 strips exactly 4" (10cm) wide from the unbleached cotton fabric and set aside for the border.

Treetop
(Lesson 1: Strips, squares, triangles and Lesson 7: Twigs and branches)

From the white fabric, cut 6 large squares (block C) of approx. 8" x 8" (20 x 20cm), 2 medium squares (block B) of approx. 6" x 6" (15 x 15cm) and 2 small squares (block A) of 4" x 4" (10 x 10cm).

From the short edge of the dark gray fabric, cut 2–3 strips, each 1½" and 1¼" (4 and 3cm) wide, and set aside for the tree trunk.

Cut strips approx. ¾" (2cm) wide and as long as possible from the remaining gray spotted fabric.

Make 2 small, 2 medium, and 6 large twig blocks (A, B, and C), as described in Lesson 7. Trim the blocks to the same size. Our 6 large blocks C were 6¾" x 6¾" (17 x 17cm), the 2 medium blocks B were 5" x 5" (13 x 13cm), and the 2 small blocks A were 3½" x 3½" (9 x 9cm) in size. Go by the size to which your blocks can be easily cut.

Sewing plan: from top to bottom
Position the blocks so that the diagonal branches point upward from the tree

Sewing plan for Four seasons: winter.

trunk. Arrange 2 blocks A, 2 blocks B, and 6 blocks C in pairs from top to bottom. Divide 2 unbleached cotton squares of approx. 2" x 2" (5 x 5cm) and 2 of approx. 4" x 4" (10 x 10cm) once, diagonally, to make 4 triangles.

Join a small unbleached cotton triangle to the top outer corner of both small blocks A to round off the tree shape. To do this, cut a corner off the block and replace it with an unbleached cotton triangle. Fold out the sewn-on triangle, press, and re-cut the block to size. Now add a 1¼" (3cm)-high unbleached cotton strip to the top edge of both blocks. Insert a ¾" (2cm)-wide dark gray strip between the 2 small blocks to make a tree trunk. Fill out the row to the right and left with unbleached cotton to a finished width of 13½" (34cm).

Add a small unbleached cotton triangle to the top outer corners of both blocks B. Insert a 1¼" (3cm)-wide dark gray tree trunk between the blocks and fill out the row of blocks to a finished width of 13½" (34cm).

Join a larger unbleached cotton triangle to the top outer corners of the 2 top blocks C. Next come 2 unaltered blocks C. Join a larger unbleached cotton triangle to the outer bottom corner of the bottom blocks C. Press the seams and insert a 1½" (4cm)-wide tree trunk in between.

Insert a 1½" (4cm)-wide tree trunk between 2 horizontal unbleached cotton rectangles.

Now join all the sections together, making sure that the tree trunk is vertical.

The tree panel should now be approx. 29½" (75cm) high and approx. 13½" (34cm) wide. Neaten the edges using a ruler and rotary cutter.

Adding a border
(Lesson 11)
Cut 4" (10cm)-wide strips of unbleached cotton and join them to the top and side edges. Join a 4" (10cm)-wide strip of white fabric to the bottom edge to make the snow.

If you'd like to, you can decorate this with lace.

Making up the quilt and quilting
(Lessons 12 and 13)
Lay the backing, batting, and pressed front panel one on top of the other. Quilt a double frame line in ecru 2" (5cm) in from the edge and fill the border with radiating lines. Quilt an ornate background pattern onto the background fabric (we used a dense stippling pattern). Quilt along the edges of the trunk, branches, and twigs using dark thread. Quilt the edges of the lace using white thread.

Binding
(Lesson 14)
Bind the basted quilt edge with a 2½" (6cm)-wide strip of gray fabric, straight-cut.

Finishing
Make a hanger casing and sew to the top edge at the back.

Four Seasons: Fall
35½" x 19½" (90 x 50cm)

For this project, it is important to use a fabric with large leaves on a light background, so that the treetop looks light and airy.

■ Materials
Fabrics
- 24" (60cm) large-print fabric of fall leaves on a light background for the treetop
- 10" (25cm) dark blue or black fabric for trunk, branches, and twigs
- 32" (80cm) unbleached cotton fabric for the background
- 4" (10cm) dark-green patterned fabric for the meadow

Other materials
- 39" x 24" (100 x 60cm) backing fabric
- 39" x 24" (100 x 60cm) batting
- quilting thread in ecru and dark blue or black
- soft pencil or chalk pencil

■ Method
Preparation
Cut 3 strips exactly 2½" (6cm) wide from the leaf-pattern fabric and set aside for the binding. Cut another 3 strips exactly 4" (10cm) wide from the unbleached cotton fabric and set aside for the border.

Treetop
(Lesson 1: Strips, squares, triangles and Lesson 7: Twigs and branches)
From the leaf-pattern fabric, cut 6 large squares (block C) of approx. 8" x 8"

(20 x 20cm) and 2 medium squares (block B) of approx. 6" x 6" (15 x 15cm). Cut a strip 1½" (4cm) and 2 strips 1¼" (3cm) wide from the short edge of the dark blue

fabric and set aside for the tree trunk. Cut strips approx. ¾" (2cm) wide and as long as possible from the remaining dark blue fabric for the branches.

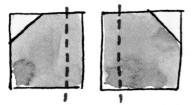

Trim 2 blocks C (top pair) by approx. 2" (5cm) along their inner edges.

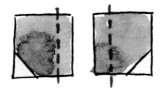

Trim 2 blocks B (bottom pair) by approx. 2" (5cm) along their inner edges.

The tree panel should now be approx. 29½" (75cm) high and approx. 13½" (34cm) wide. Neaten the edges using a ruler and rotary cutter.

Make 2 medium and 6 large twig blocks (B and C), as described in Lesson 7. Trim the blocks to the same size. Our 6 large blocks C were 6¾" x 6¾" (17 x 17cm), and the 2 medium blocks B were 4¾" (12cm) high and 4" (10cm) wide.

Arrange the 6 large blocks C and the 2 blocks B in pairs to make a tree shape. Divide 2 unbleached cotton squares of 4¾" x 4¾" (12 x 12cm), one of 4" x 4" (10 x 10cm), and another of 3¼" x 3¼" (8 x 8cm) in half diagonally to form triangles.

Sewing plan from top to bottom

Using the larger triangles as a template, cut the top outer corners from the first 2 large blocks and insert an unbleached cotton triangle in each gap. Trim 1¼" (3cm) from the edges of the block facing the trunk and insert a ¾" (2cm)-wide tree trunk in between. Extend the block to the left and right with strips of unbleached cotton fabric (approx. 1½"–2" [4–5cm] wide).

For the second pair, cut the 2 top outer corners and insert the 2 smallest triangles. For the third set of blocks, replace the 2 bottom outer corners with medium-size unbleached cotton triangles. Trim the

blocks to shape. Insert the 1¼" (3cm)-wide strip of tree trunk between the 2 sets of blocks.

For the 2 bottom blocks B, cut the 2 bottom outer corners and insert 2 of the larger triangles. Trim off 1¼" (3cm) from the edges nearest the trunk and add a strip of unbleached cotton to the bottom edges, the same width as the block. The 2 sections should now be approx. 8" (20cm) long. Insert the 1½" (4cm)-wide strip of trunk in between the blocks. Extend the sides of bottom blocks B with unbleached cotton fabric to make all the sections the same width. Join up the sections to make the tree.

Adding a border
(Lesson 11)
Cut 4" (10cm)-wide strips of unbleached cotton and join them to the long sides and along the top edge of the panel. Join a 4" (10cm)-wide strip of green patterned fabric to the bottom edge to make the meadow.

Making up the quilt and quilting
(Lessons 12 and 13)
Lay the backing, batting, and pressed front panel one on top of the other. Quilt a double frame line in ecru 1¼" (3cm) in from the edge and fill the border with radiating lines. Quilt an ornate background pattern onto the background fabric (we used a dense stippling pattern). Quilt up and down the trunk and branches with black thread. Quilt vertical lines on the "meadow" using dark thread.

Binding
(Lesson 14)
Bind the basted quilt edge with the 2½" (6cm)-wide strip of leaf-pattern fabric.

Finishing
Make a hanger casing and sew to the top edge at the back.

Sewing plan for the fall tree.

Four Seasons: Spring
35½" x 19½" (90 x 50cm)

The foliage on our tree in spring is not so dense, creating a more varied shape and yet it is exactly the same height as the others, so the trees for all four seasons can be displayed together.

■ Materials
Fabrics
- 20" (50cm) fabric with foliage printed on a light blue background for the treetop and binding
- 10" (25cm) dark brown plain fabric for the trunk, twigs, and branches
- 32" (80cm) unbleached cotton fabric for the background
- 4" (10cm) green and beige striped fabric for the meadow

Other materials
- 39" x 24" (100 x 60cm) backing fabric
- 39" x 24" (100 x 60cm) batting
- quilting thread in ecru, green, and dark brown
- soft pencil

■ Method
Preparation
Cut 3 strips exactly 2½" (6cm) wide from the foliage fabric and set aside for the binding. Cut another 3 strips exactly 4" (10cm) wide from unbleached cotton fabric and set aside for the border.

Treetop
(Lesson 1: Strips, squares, triangles and Lesson 7: Twigs and branches)
From the foliage-pattern fabric, cut 4 large squares (block C) of approx.

8" x 8" (20 x 20cm), 2 medium squares (block B) of approx. 6" x 6" (15 x 15cm), and 4 small squares (block A) of approx. 4" x 4" (10 x 10cm).

Cut 2 strips 1½" (4cm) wide and 2 strips 1¼" (3cm) wide from the short edge of the brown fabric and set aside for the tree trunk. Cut strips ½"–¾" (1.5–2cm) wide and as long as possible from the remaining fabric for the branches.

From the squares of foliage-pattern fabric, make 4 small, 2 medium, and 4 large twig blocks (A, B, and C), as described in Lesson 7. Neaten the edges of the blocks.

Sewing plan from top to bottom

Arrange the blocks to make a tree shape. Refer to the sewing plan or find an arrangement that you like. The blocks should not be arranged symmetrically or

Sewing plan for Four seasons: spring.

the treetop will look too formal. Divide 3 unbleached cotton squares of 4" x 4" (10 x 10cm) in half diagonally to make 6 triangles and divide 2 unbleached cotton squares of 2½" x 2½" (6 x 6cm) to make 4 triangles.

Join a small unbleached cotton triangle to the top left-hand corner of the left-hand block A and an approx. 1½" (4cm)-wide strip to the bottom edge. Join a small unbleached cotton triangle to the bottom right-hand corner of the right-hand block A and add an approx. 1½" (4cm)-wide strip to the top edge. Insert a strip of tree trunk between the 2 pieces and extend the section with unbleached cotton fabric to a total width of 12½" (32cm).

Join the medium unbleached cotton triangles to the outer top corners of the 2 blocks B. Insert the strip of tree trunk and extend the section with unbleached cotton fabric to a total width of 12½" (32cm). Join a large unbleached cotton triangle to the outer top and bottom corners of the 4 blocks C (see illustration). Join the 2 pairs of blocks C and then insert the strip of tree trunk in between.

For the bottom left-hand block A, join a small unbleached cotton triangle to the bottom left-hand corner and an approx. 1¼" (3cm)-wide strip to the top edge. For the bottom right-hand block A, join a small unbleached cotton triangle to the right-hand bottom corner and an approx. 2½" (6cm)-wide strip to the top edge. Extend both sections to approx. 10" (25cm) in height with unbleached cotton fabric. Insert the tree trunk in between the pieces and extend the trunk to the same width as the other sections.

The tree trunk should be 1½" (4cm) wide at the bottom, 1¼" (3cm) wide in the center, and ¾" (2cm) wide at the top. Join up the sections to make the tree.

The tree panel should now be approx. 29½" (75cm) high and approx. 3½" (34cm) wide. Neaten the edges using a ruler and rotary cutter.

Adding a border

(Lesson 11)
Cut 4" (10cm)-wide strips of unbleached cotton and join them to the long sides and along the top edge of the panel. Join a 4" (10cm)-wide strip of green/beige striped fabric to the bottom edge to make the meadow.

Making up the quilt and quilting

(Lessons 12 and 13)
Lay the backing, batting, and pressed front panel one on top of the other. Quilt a double frame line in ecru 1¼" (3cm) in from the edge and fill the border with radiating lines. Quilt an ornate background pattern onto the background fabric (we used a dense stippling pattern). Quilt up and down the trunk and branches with brown thread. Quilt vertical lines on the "meadow" using green thread.

Binding

(Lesson 14)
Bind the basted quilt edge with the 2½" (6cm)-wide strip of foliage-patterned fabric.

Finishing

Make a hanger casing and sew to the top edge at the back.

Four Seasons: Summer
35½" x 19½" (90 x 50cm)

I have chosen a citrus tree to represent summer. I would have liked to make the binding in the same citrus fruit-patterned fabric as the foliage, but it ran out so I had to use a different one; the main thing is that the color matches.

▨ Materials
Fabrics
- 16" (40cm) fabric with a pattern of citrus fruits, flowers, and leaves on a light background for the treetop and binding
- 8" (20cm) maroon-colored fabric for the trunk, twigs, and branches
- 1¼ yd. (1m) unbleached cotton fabric for the background
- 4" (10cm) grass-green fabric for the meadow

Other materials
- 39" x 24" (100 x 60cm) backing fabric
- 39" x 24" (100 x 60cm) batting
- quilting thread in ecru, dark brown, and green
- soft pencil

▨ Method
Preparation
Cut 3 strips exactly 2½" (6cm) wide from the citrus fruit-pattern fabric and set aside for the binding (assuming you have enough!). Cut another 3 strips exactly 4" (10cm) wide from unbleached cotton fabric and set aside for the border.

Treetop
(Lesson 1: Strips, squares, triangles and Lesson 7: Twigs and branches)
Cut 4 squares (block C) of approx. 8" x 8" (20 x 20cm) from the citrus

fruit-pattern fabric. Cut 3 strips 1½" (4cm) wide and 1 strip 1¼" (3cm) wide from the short edge of the maroon-colored fabric and set aside for the tree trunk. Cut strips ¾" (2cm) wide and as long as possible from the remaining fabric for the branches.

Make 4 twig blocks, as described in Lesson 7. Trim the blocks to exactly 6¾" x 6¾" (17 x 17cm).

Sewing plan from top to bottom

Join a 1¼" (3cm)-wide maroon-colored strip between the 2 top blocks and a 1½" (4cm)-wide maroon-colored strip between the 2 bottom blocks for the tree trunk. Assemble the sections to make the treetop.

Cut 2 squares approx. 4¾" x 4¾" (12 x 12cm) from the unbleached cotton fabric and divide each in half diagonally to make 4 triangles. Using the triangles as templates, cut the 4 corners of the treetop off diagonally and join an unbleached cotton triangle to each.

Join the remaining 1½" (4cm)-wide maroon-colored strips to make the tree trunk. Cut to 14½" (37cm) in length. Join a 6¾" (17cm)-wide strip of unbleached cotton fabric to the left and right sides of the trunk. Join section to treetop. Join four ¾" (12cm) strips of unbleached cotton fabric to the top of the tree. The tree panel should now be approx. 34" (86cm) high and 13½" (34cm) wide.

Neaten the edges using a ruler and rotary cutter.

Adding a border
(Lesson 11)
Cut 4" (10cm)-wide strips of unbleached cotton and join them to the long sides of the panel. Join a 4" (10cm)-wide strip of green grass fabric to the bottom edge to make the meadow.

Making up the quilt and quilting
(Lessons 12 and 13)
Lay the backing, batting, and pressed front panel one on top of the other. Quilt a double frame line in ecru 2" (5cm) in from the edge and fill the border with radiating lines. Quilt an ornate background pattern onto the background fabric (we used a dense stippling pattern). Quilt up and down the trunk and branches with brown thread. Quilt vertical lines on the "grass" using green thread.

Binding
(Lesson 14)
Bind the basted quilt edge with the 2½" (6cm)-wide strip of citrus fruit-pattern fabric.

Finishing
Make a hanger casing and sew to the top edge at the back.

Sewing plan Four seasons: summer.

Winter Wonderland
90½" x 84½" (230 x 215cm)

Different shades of white combine to make a pleasing picture. You could recycle the lace edging of vintage linen—it doesn't matter if it is a bit worn or has a few holes in it. I can hear the lacemakers complaining already but surely it's better for fine old lace to be cut up and used on a quilt rather than letting it lie forever at the bottom of the sewing box.

■ Materials
Fabrics
- 3¼ yd. (3m) ecru and/or unbleached cotton (or 2¼ yd. [2m] fabric with a width of 60" [150cm]) for trunks, branches, accent strip, and binding
- 8¾ yd. (8m) white fabric (or 6½ yd. [6m] fabric with a width of 60" [150cm]), or a suitable amount of white bedlinen for the background

Other materials
- needle/crocheted and bobbin lace (damaged pieces are fine)
- 99" x 91" (250 x 230cm) backing fabric
- 99" x 91" (250 x 230cm) batting
- quilting thread in white and ecru
- soft pencil

■ Method
Preparation
Cut 4 strips 2" (5cm) wide from the ecru fabric for the accent strip and 10 strips 2½" (6cm) wide for the binding and set aside.

7 trees for the winter wonderland
(Lesson 7: Twigs and branches)
Cut 26 squares (block A) of 4" x 4" (10 x 10cm), 26 squares (block B) 6" x 6" (15 x 15cm), and 16 squares

(block C) 8" x 8" (20 x 20cm) from the white fabric. From the ecru fabric, cut a quantity of strips 1½" (4cm) wide and 1¼" (3cm) wide for the tree trunks, and strips ¾" (2cm) wide for the branches.

Make the twig blocks, as described in Lesson 7.

You will need:
26 x block A (small) 4" x 4" (10 x 10cm) squares, 3½" x 3½" (9 x 9cm) when trimmed
26 x block B (medium) 6" x 6" (15 x 15cm) squares, 4¾" x 4¾" (12 x 12cm) when trimmed
16 x block C (large) 8" x 8" (20 x 20cm) squares, 6¾" x 6¾" (17 x 17cm) when trimmed

Arrange the blocks in pairs and insert a tree trunk between each pair, using a wider strip for each section as you go down the trunk. Choose different combinations and different tree sizes so that the forest looks natural.

A   B   C

26 x block A, 3½" x 3½" (9 x 9cm)
26 x block B, 4¾" x 4¾" (12 x 12cm)
16 x block C, 6¾" x 6¾" (17 x 17cm)

Our trees were assembled as follows (arranged from top to bottom, with the trunk between each pair of blocks):

Tree 1: AA, BB, CC, BB, AA
Tree 2: AA, BB, AA
Tree 3: AA, BB, CC, AA
Tree 4: as for tree 3, but placed a little lower
Tree 5: as for tree 2
Tree 6: as for tree 1
Tree 7: AA, 2 x CC, BB

Sewing plan for row of trees
Fill the gaps between the trees with white fabric (see dotted lines in the illustration) and insert the wide tree trunk sections extending all the way to the ground. Make 7 complete trees, as shown, extending the background fabric until all the trees are the same height. Join all the trees side by side and add a strip of white fabric approx. 4" (10cm) wide to both sides at the same height as the trees. Join a 2" (5cm) strip of white fabric along the entire bottom edge of the piece.

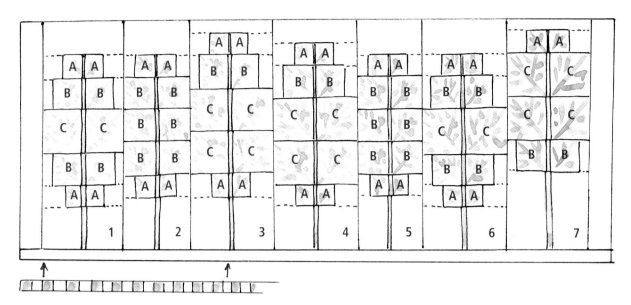

1 2 3 4 5 6 7

Place line of 7 trees with different block arrangements side by side. All the tree sections should be the same height. Extend the row of trees to the left and right with strips of white fabric and add a long white fabric strip and the accent strip to the bottom.

Accent strip
(Lesson 9)

Cut 3 white fabric strips exactly 2" (5cm) wide. Join these to the three 2" (5cm) ecru fabric strips you set aside earlier. Make an accent strip (see Lesson 9) long enough to run across the entire width of the quilt. Join the accent strip to the bottom edge of the white strip under the row of trees.

Working with lace

Trim off the lace from old bed pillows or sheets, or you could use needle or crocheted lace borders from old table linen. Sew the lace pieces individually or in pairs (depending on width) onto strips of white fabric approx. 4¾"–5" (12–13cm) wide (for the bottom snowfield) and/or strips approx. 2½" (6cm) wide (for the snowflakes). Try not to stretch the lace as you sew it. Use white or ecru thread and long, straight stitches as you sew across the lace pieces. These seams will be almost

invisible. For narrow embroidered lace pieces with fabric edges, fold the raw fabric edge under and stitch close to the edge. You could also use the decorative stitches on the sewing machine for this, if you prefer

Follow the shapes of arches and edges to strengthen them. Press the lace pieces and remove any marked and damaged areas.

Snowdrifts for the ground

Cut squares of 4¾" x 4¾" (12 x 12cm) from the wider lace strip (how many you make will depend on how much lace you have available). We arranged lace squares and large, plain white squares in a checkerboard pattern (a total of 72 squares of 4¾" x 4¾" [12 x 12cm]), rows of 21 squares (see Lesson 10) and join this section to the bottom edge of the accent strip.

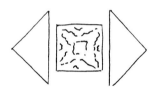

Extend a lace square 2½" x 2½"(6 x 6cm) with triangles. Trim off the excess corners.

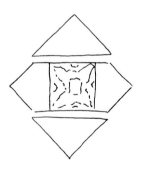

Add triangles to opposite sides. Trim the block to a square 4¾" x 4¾"(12 x 12cm).

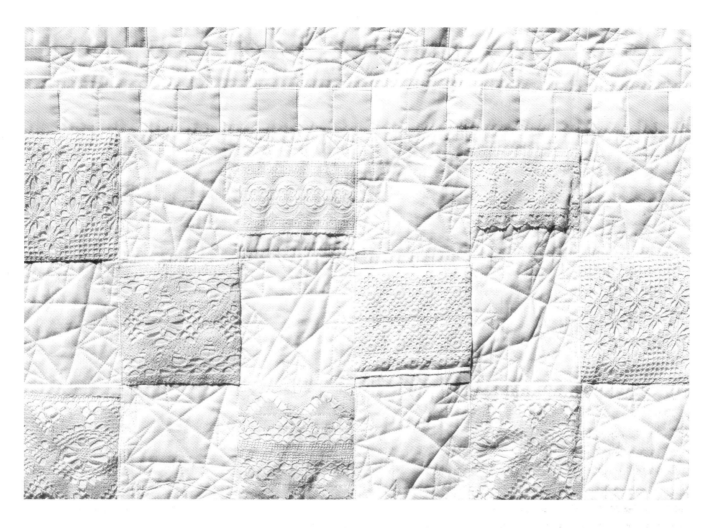

Snowflakes for the sky

Cut squares of 2" x 2" (5 x 5cm) from the narrow lace strips. Cut squares of white fabric approx. 4¾" x 4¾" (12 x 12cm) and divide them in half diagonally to make triangles. Join a centered triangle to the left and right sides of each lace square and trim off the excess edges of the triangle in line with the square. Join 2 more triangles to the opposite edges of the lace square. Press the block and cut it to exactly 4¾" x 4¾" (12 x 12cm). You can also make monograms and small lace motifs in the same way.

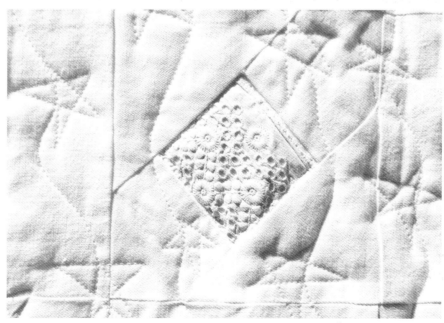

The number of lace blocks will depend on how much lace you can find. Extend the sky area with white fabric squares cut to exactly 4¾" x 4¾" (12 x 12cm). We arranged snowflake blocks and white squares in a checkerboard pattern with an area of plain white squares above the central tree. You will need to make 11 rows of 21 squares each for this area (Lesson 10). Join the section to the row of trees. Trim the side edges straight.

Making up the quilt and quilting
(Lessons 12 and 13)
Lay the backing, batting, and pressed front section one on top of the other.

Quilt lots of stars onto the background: you could, for example, "hang" a row of small five-pointed stars in a vertical wavy line. Quilt arcs of stars in the center above the trees and large stars onto the white background squares; you could also quilt small stars between the points of each large star. Using ecru-colored thread, quilt around the snowdrift and snowflake squares, along the trunks, branches, and twigs of the trees, and along all the seams of the accent strip.

Binding
(Lesson 14)
Bind the basted quilt edge with a straight-cut strip of ecru fabric 2½" (6cm) wide.

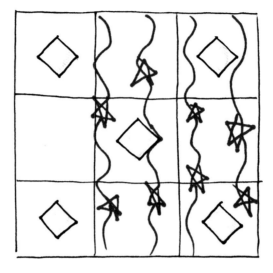

Snowflake blocks alternating with white squares. Quilting suggestion for the sky.

Quilting suggestion for the trees.

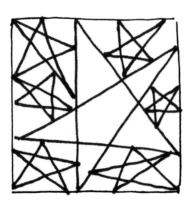

Quilting suggestion for the white squares (4¾" x 4¾" [12 x 12cm]) in the bottom part of the quilt.

Desert Dwellings
90½" x 84¼" (230 x 214cm)

Bedouin storage huts are made from clay, with small staircases rising to little arched doorways often framed with a decorative white border. The diagonal flights of steps are perfect for the composition of a medallion quilt, and we have added a horde of little quilted geckos scampering across the surrounding desert.

■ Materials
Fabrics

- 10" (25cm) (long quarters) of 30 different light to mid-brown sand colors, plain or lightly patterned, for the desert area, the steps, and the door blocks
- 1½ yd. (1.30m) unbleached cotton fabric for the door frames, the piping around the inner doorway (or use white fabric), and the binding
- 3 yd. (2.60m) plain, dark brown fabric for the backing for the steps, the piping on the doorways, the inner doorway, and the binding

Other materials

- 99" x 91" (250 x 230cm) backing fabric
- 99" x 91" (250 x 230cm) batting
- quilting thread in light, mid-, and dark brown shades
- 3 pieces of strong card, approx. 10" x 10" (25 x 25cm), for the templates for the steps, doors, and geckos (if necessary)
- graph paper and glue (if necessary)
- water-soluble marker pen for the light fabrics
- chalk pencil for the dark fabrics
- gecko quilting pattern (9" [23cm] long, see page 102)

■ Method
Preparation

Cut 40 squares of 10" x 10" (25 x 25cm) from the darker shades of sand-colored fabric and set aside. Divide the "long quarters" of sand-colored fabric in half down the center to make rectangles approx. 22" (55cm) long.

40 Desert blocks

(Lesson 6: Curved seams)
You will need around 40 rectangles of fabric 10" x approx. 22" (25 x approx. 55cm) (= half the width of the strip of fabric cut from selvage to selvage). Place 3 different pieces of fabric one on top of the other, right sides up, and make 2 curving cuts down their length. Swap over the colors and join up the pieces along their long sides. Trim the strips to the same size; ours were exactly 8¼" (21cm) high. (This size matches the dimensions of the squares in the center section, which should be trimmed to exactly 8¼" x 8¼" [21 x 21cm]).

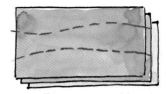

Lay 3 different desert fabrics one on top of the other, rights sides up. Make 2 curving cuts through all 3 layers

Rearrange the pieces so that there are 3 different colors in each block. Join up the seams and press.

20 outer sets of steps

The steps can be drawn freehand directly onto the fabric. If you prefer to work with a template, draw a set of 1¼" (3cm)-high steps (6 small squares on the diagonal) on a 10" x 10" (25 x 25cm) piece of graph paper. Stick the graph paper onto a piece of strong card and cut out the steps.

Cut 10 squares of dark brown fabric approx. 10" x 10" (25 x 25cm) and choose 10 of the sand-colored fabric squares you set aside. With right sides facing, place a dark brown and a sand-colored square together, and draw the steps diagonally from corner to corner. Sew a ¼" (0.5cm) seam along both sides parallel to the pencil line. Cut the fabrics along the pencil line. Trim off the corners of the steps at an angle and clip into the angles almost up to the seams. Turn both sets of steps right side out and press the hemmed edges carefully. Make 20 sets of steps in this way.

3 long and 3 short inner sets of steps

To make the 3 long sets of steps within the settlement, you will need 3 of the approx. 10" x 10" (25 x 25cm) sand-colored squares that you set aside. Place one of the outer sets of steps on each square, with the lighter fabric facing upward and the steps running diagonally across the square. Make sure any raw edges of the steps lie outside the fabric square. Pin in place and stitch along the edge of the steps with light brown thread. Carefully remove the 2 layers of excess fabric behind the steps and use them to make a set of shorter steps: with right sides facing, place the pieces of fabric together and sew a ¼" (0.5cm) seam along the step edges. Turn this short set of steps right side out, as described above, and set aside. Make 3 long and 3 short inner sets of steps.

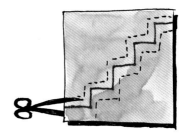

Place a sand-colored square on a dark brown square of fabric, right sides facing, and draw a set of steps. Stitch a ¼" (0.5cm) seam to the left and right of the line, then cut along the line.

Trim off the corners of the steps at an angle and clip into the angles right up to the seam. Turn the steps right side out and press.

Edge stitch the steps to a sand-colored square of fabric. Carefully remove the 2 excess layers of fabric behind the steps and use the pieces to make a shorter set of steps.

20 door blocks
(Lesson 8: Piping techniques)

For the backgrounds you will need 20 of the approx. 10" x 10" (25 x 25cm) sand-colored squares that you set aside. For the doors you will need 20 dark brown and 20 unbleached cotton rectangles of approx. 8" x 7" (20 x 17cm), 20 white squares of approx. 6" x 6" (15 x 15cm), and 20 dark brown rectangles of approx. 4" x 6" (10 x 15cm). Center a dark brown rectangle vertically on a mid-brown square, right sides facing and bottom edges aligned. Draw an arch 5½"–6" (14–15cm) high and about 4"–4¼" (10–11cm) wide at the bottom. The arch should be wider at the bottom; you can make a template from card for this if you prefer. Sew along the pencil line, then cut out the archway just inside the line, leaving a seam allowance. Clip the seam allowances and fold the dark brown fabric back through the archway leaving a narrow piped edge. Press the edge.

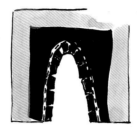

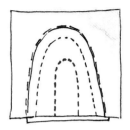

Clip the seam allowances. Fold the dark brown fabric back through the opening, leaving a narrow piped edge. Flatten the edge and press.

Draw a smaller arch on the back and sew along the line. Turn the block over so the front is uppermost.

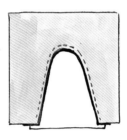

Place an unbleached cotton rectangle behind the opening and stitch around the edges of the arch. Trim off the excess fabric at the back.

Cut away the fabric inside the smaller arch and clip the seam allowance. Fold the white fabric to the back through the opening. Flatten the edges and press.

Place a dark brown rectangle of fabric onto a sand-colored square, right sides facing and with bottom edges aligned. Draw an arch, sew along the line, and cut away both layers of fabric from inside the arch.

With right sides facing, place a white unbleached cotton rectangle over the arch. Pin in place and turn the block over so that the back is uppermost.

Place a small rectangle of dark brown fabric behind the arch and stitch along the white edge from the right side.

Place a piece of unbleached cotton fabric approx. 8" x 7" (20 x 17cm) behind the archway, both right sides facing up. Pin the archway in place and stitch along the edge with light-colored thread. Trim off the excess fabric.

Place a square of unbleached cotton fabric approx. 5½" x 5½" (14 x 14cm) over the archway, right sides facing. Turn the block over and draw the inner arch door onto the back (drawing on the back makes it easier to center the arch). The inner arch should be 4" (10cm) high and 2" (5cm) along the bottom edge. You can make a card template for this inner arch as well if you like. Sew along the line and cut out the material inside the arch, leaving a seam allowance. Clip the seam allowance and fold the white fabric back through the archway. Flatten the edge and press.

Finally, cut rectangles of approx. 4" x 6" (10 x 15cm) from the dark brown fabric and place them behind the inner arches. Stitch around the edge of the arch with white thread and trim the excess fabric from the back. Press the seam allowances of the dark fabric so that they do not show through to the front. Make 20 door blocks with a white frame and cut them all to exactly 8¼" x 8¼"(21 x 21cm) (= same depth as the desert blocks).

Sewing plan

Join as many desert sections as you need to make up a width of 87" (220cm). As you join each row, make sure that the vertical seams are offset from those of the preceding row, like a brick wall. Cut off any excess desert sections and use these to fill other rows; this will make sure you avoid vertical seams that align.

Sewing plan, quilting suggestion and binding.

Make the appropriate end-piece for desert sections that border the central medallion using a diagonal set of steps to form the edge. These may run toward the top or the bottom on the right or left-hand side. Stitch along the edges of the steps. Carefully trim off the 2 layers of fabric behind the blocks. You will be able to make additional small sets of steps from these excess fabric pieces.

Lay out all the blocks on a sufficiently large surface. Distribute the 20 door blocks and the 3 step blocks around the

medallion. Sew a few small sets of steps in any arrangement you like onto the door blocks of the central medallion. You can place the steps at the top, the bottom, or left or right; just three or four steps are often enough to liven up the block. Don't forget to trim the excess layers of fabric from behind the steps here as well. After sewing the steps into place, you will have to trim the blocks to shape again.

Follow the sewing plan or find another arrangement that you like. First, join up the individual rows and then join the rows together to make the quilt front. The total width of the quilt should be 87" (220cm).

From top to bottom:

1st row: desert blocks, complete row

2nd row: desert blocks, complete row, shifted along by half a block

3rd row: desert blocks, steps to the left, steps to the right, desert blocks

4th row: desert blocks, steps to the left, 2 door blocks, steps to the right, desert blocks

5th row: desert blocks, steps to the left, 4 door blocks, steps to the right, desert blocks

6th row: desert blocks, steps to the left, 2 door blocks, inner step block, 3 door blocks, steps to the right, desert blocks

7th row: desert blocks, steps to the left, 3 door blocks, 2 inner step blocks, 1 door block, steps to the right, desert blocks

8th row: desert blocks, steps to the left, 4 door blocks, steps to the right, desert blocks

9th row: desert blocks, steps to the left, 2 door blocks, steps to the right, desert blocks

10th row: as row 3

11th row: as row 2

12th row: as row 2

Enlarge the gecko quilt template to 9" (23cm) (from head to tip of tail).

Making a gecko template

Our geckos were approx. 9" (23cm) long. Enlarge the template on page 102 or find a gecko picture on the internet. If you do this, choose a photo where the complete animal is shown from above, print it out and trace the outline, enlarging it to the size you need.

Make a template out of a piece of card. Trace around the outline with water-soluble marker onto the front of the quilt, turning and rotating the template so the reptiles appear in different positions.

Quilting

Using a water-soluble marker, draw geckos and wavy double lines (approx. ¾" [2cm] apart) at handbreadth intervals across the full width of the quilt, interrupting the lines when you reach the geckos. Machine quilting: quilt the outlines of the geckos and along the double lines. Fill the large areas between the lines with pebbles or another dense background pattern. Within the central medallion, quilt along the block seams and along the lines of the steps at a distance of approx. ½" (1cm). Make some dense patterns with dark brown thread in the doorways. Hand quilting: if you are quilting by hand, leave out the pebble

pattern and the dense patterns in the doorways. Finally, wash off the water-soluble lines using a spray.

Binding

(Lesson 9: Accent Strips)

Bind the quilt with an accent strip. To make this, cut 12 dark brown and 12 unbleached cotton fabric strips, each 2" (5cm) wide, and join them along their long sides, alternating the colors. Cut two ½" (6.5cm)-wide sections and join these to make a narrow strip approx. 10½–11yd. (9.5–10m) long. Bind the basted quilt edge with the accent strip, making straight corners.

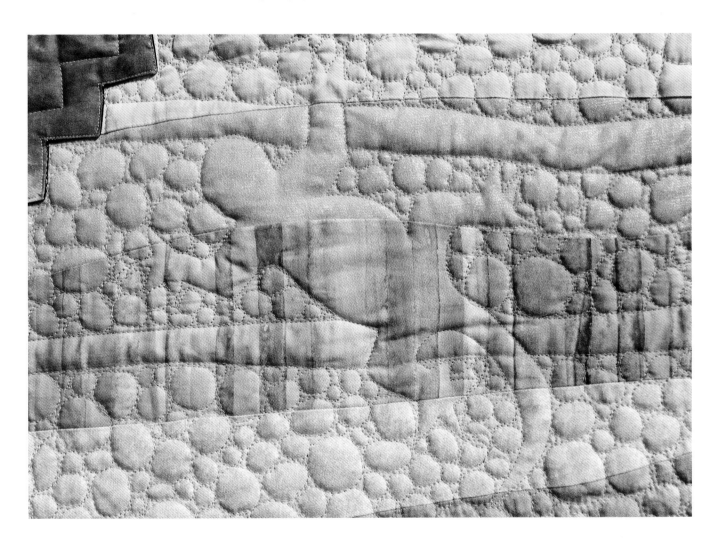

Child's Rucksack
approx. 10" x 12" (25 x 30cm)

All a child needs to turn a boring walk into an exciting adventure is a water bottle and an apple in this useful little rucksack.

■ Materials
Fabrics

- 20" (50cm) brown patterned fabric for the outside and the shoulder strap holders
- 1¼ yd. (1m) orange patterned fabric for the lining, the inside pocket (if you make one), and the binding around the flap edge (alternatively use ready-made bias tape, in which case you will need only 20" [50cm] of fabric)
- 2 scraps of green fabric (4" x 6" [10 x 15cm]) for the small tree on the flap
- scrap of beige fabric (2" x 5" [5 x 12cm]) for the button loop

Other materials

- approx. 20" x 20" (50 x 50cm) batting
- sheet of paper approx. 20" x 10" (50 x 25cm) for the template
- approx. 14" (35cm) elastic for the top edge
- safety pin to insert the elastic
- 1 button, approx. ¾" (2cm) in diameter
- 1 yd. (1m) black webbing, 1¼" (3cm) wide, for the straps
- 4 black plastic buckles, 1½" (3.5cm) wide, to hold and adjust the straps
- 1½ yd. (1.30m) bias tape, 1¼" (3cm) wide, in a color to match the lining (if required)

■ Method
Preparation

To make the base of the rucksack, cut a paper template with the following dimensions: total height 19" (48cm), width 8" (20cm). Round off the top and bottom edges for the flap and base, working freehand or using a plate as a template. The rucksack front is made as a separate rectangle, 8¾" x 17" (22 x 43cm).

Making the rucksack front

Cut a rectangle of 17" x 8¾" (43 x 22cm) from the brown patterned fabric and the batting, and a rectangle of 17" x 10¾" (43 x 27cm) from the lining fabric. Place both pieces of fabric together, wrong sides facing, with the batting in between. The lining fabric should overlap at the top edge by 2" (5cm); this will form the casing for the elastic.

Quilt a simple pattern across the rectangle with your sewing machine (we used diagonal lines) and neaten the side and bottom edges with zigzag stitches.

Fold the excess piece of lining fabric over the top edge of the rucksack front. Fold under a ½" (1cm) hem and stitch along the edge to make a casing. Using a safety pin, thread the elastic through the casing and secure the ends of the elastic firmly to the edges of the casing.

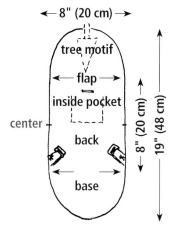

Make a paper template. Trace the markings onto the front.

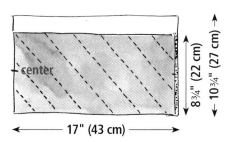

Rucksack front: layer the outer fabric, batting, and lining fabric together, with the wrong sides facing the batting and the lining fabric overlapping at the top by 2" (5cm). Quilt and neaten the edges with zigzag stitches.

Fold the lining fabric over the raw edge, fold under a narrow hem and stitch along the edge. Thread the elastic through the casing and secure the ends firmly.

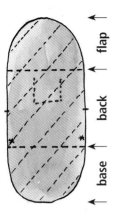

Cut the back section (base, back, and flap) to shape. Place the layers on top of one another and quilt as with the front section, neatening the edges with zigzag stitches. Transfer the markings.

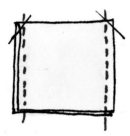

To make the inside pocket, fold a rectangle of fabric in half lengthways, right sides facing, and join the side seams. Trim off the corners of the seam allowance and turn right side out.

Pin the inside pocket securely to the inside of the rucksack with the folded edge at the top. Fold the raw bottom edges under and sew around all the edges, leaving the top edge open.

Making the back of the rucksack

This section includes the base, the back, and the flap. Use the template to cut the outer fabric, batting, and lining fabric. Layer up the fabrics with the wrong sides nearest the batting. Quilt across the entire piece (we used diagonal lines) and neaten the outer edges with zigzag stitches.

If you wish, you can make a small inside pocket from a rectangle of fabric 5" x 9" (12 x 22cm). Fold the rectangle in half lengthways, right sides facing, and join up the sides. Trim off the corners of the seam allowances at an angle. Turn the pocket right side out and fold under the raw edges. Pin the pocket to the inside of the rucksack; the closed top edge of the rectangle should be approx. 7" (18cm) below the top curve. Stitch along the sides and the bottom edge, making sure you secure the beginning and end of the line of stitches firmly.

To make the 2 shoulder strap holders, cut 2 strips of 2" x 6" (5 x 15cm) and fold the long edges in toward the center, so that they overlap slightly. Stitch securely with a continuous seam running the length of the strap. Push each strap through one of the buckles and fold it in half. Pin the loops to the back section of the rucksack, about ½" (1cm) above the point where the base corners will be. The side without a seam should be on the inside and the side with the seam should face outward; the strap holders should be angled slightly upward. Trim the ends in line with the outer edge of the back section.

Make the shoulder strap holders from strips of fabric.

Push the strap holders through the buckles and pin them to the outside of the back section at the points marked on the template with a *.

Tip

The buckles for the shoulder straps don't actually need a center bar, but these were the only ones we had to hand.

With right sides facing, join the side edges of the front to the center of the back section, with the gathered edge facing up toward the flap. Make sure the shoulder strap holders are secured in the seam.

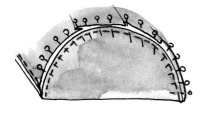

Fold up the base, pin to the bottom edge of the front section and join. You may have to ease the fabric of the front section in places, to make a perfect fit.

Bind the inner edges and flap of the rucksack with bias tape.

Making up the rucksack

With right sides facing, join the side edges of the front to the sides of the base section in the center, making sure you include the shoulder strap holders in the seam. With right sides facing, fold up the curved base section and pin to the bottom edge of the front section. Ease the fabric of the front with a few little folds in the bottom edge if necessary and close up the seam.

Finishing the edges

Cut 1¼" (3cm)-wide bias strips from the lining fabric and join them to form one strip approx. 52" (130cm) long. Fold the bias tape in half lengthways, wrong sides facing, and press. Open out the strip and, with right sides facing, sew the strip around the outer edges of the rucksack neatened with zigzag stitches, i.e. the flap and the inner edges. Fold the binding over the raw edges, fold under a hem, and sew the folded edge to the inside of the rucksack using lockstitches. Make sure that the ends of the bias tape are tucked away on the inside of the rucksack (e.g. at a corner of the base). Turn the rucksack right sides out.

> **Tip**
> You can also make this rucksack from a small practice quilt (minimum size 20" x 20" [50 x 50cm]). If you decide to do this, sew the casing for the elastic from an additional 2" (5cm)-wide strip of fabric.

Sewing on the straps

Push one end of the webbing through both openings of a buckle, as shown. Guide the end through the buckle attached to the rucksack and thread it around the bar of the first buckle. Pull the end through and join it to make a loop approx. 1¼" (3cm) below the buckle, sewing over this several times to secure firmly.

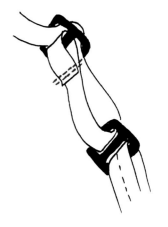

Push the strap through the buckles and secure the end very firmly.

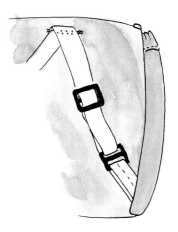

Fold the center of the strap and secure very firmly to the top edge of the rucksack, making sure not to sew up the inside pocket by mistake.

Make the other end of the shoulder straps in the same way, making sure it doesn't get twisted. Find the center of the webbing and make a 90° fold in it. Place the fold at the top edge of the rucksack, just below the fold of the flap and attach it securely with several rows of stitching, making sure you don't accidentally sew up the inside pocket at the same time.

Decorating the flap

Make a button loop from a strip of beige fabric approx. 2" (5cm) wide and 5" (12cm) long. Fold in a hem along both the long edges of the strip and press. With wrong sides together, fold the strip in half along its length and stitch together along the folded edges. Fold the strip into a loop and pin it in place on the flap; the ends should lie side by side rather than on top of one another and the loop should extend approx. 1" (2.5cm) beyond the flap.

Make a small appliqué tree motif (Lesson 8) approx. 3¼" (8cm) in height and 2½" (6cm) wide and sew onto onto the flap, using the bottom edge to cover the raw edges of the button loop, which forms its trunk. Stitch across the button loop a few times, level with the edge of the flap.

Tip
You could also appliqué a leaf motif instead of a tree; the button loop would then form the stem.

Shorten the loop with a horizontal seam so that the button just fits through. Fold the flap over the front of the rucksack to ascertain the position of the button; sew the button in place.

Make a button loop from a strip of beige fabric.

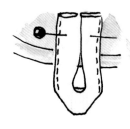

Make a loop and pin it in place on the edge of the flap.

With right sides facing, place 2 pieces of green fabric together and cut out a small tree. Trim off the corners of the seam allowance, make a slit in the backing, and turn the tree right sides out through the slit. Press.

Sew the appliqué tree onto the flap, covering the ends of the button loop. Sew the loop securely to the flap and shorten the hole to match the size of the button.

Colors of the Fall
96½" x 84½" (245 x 215cm)

We photographed this large, colorful quilt in the Grunewald forest near Berlin, surrounded by crowds of inquisitive passersby. The bright batik fabrics give a flavor of the beautiful colors that can be seen in New England as late summer turns to fall, but they're just as beautiful here in the Allgäu.

■ Materials
Fabrics
- 10" (25cm) each of 30 different batiks, plain, and lightly patterned fabrics in the widest range of brilliant fall colors you can find, including yellow, green, brown, purple, orange, red, for the treetops, branches and trunks (total length approx. 9yd. [8m])
- 8" (20cm) light turquoise for the sky in the top row
- 5" (12cm) dark turquoise for the earth in the bottom row

Other materials
- 102" x 91" (260 x 230cm) backing fabric
- 102" x 91" (260 x 230cm) batting
- 10¼ yd. (9.40m) wine-red bias tape
- variegated quilting thread in fall colors
- triangular ruler (if necessary)
- large pin board on which you can lay out the whole quilt

Cutting guide
10" (25cm) fabric is enough to make 10 rectangles = 10 trees. Allow 2 narrow strips per tree for branches and trunk.

■ Method
214 trees
Cut at least 230 rectangles 10" (25cm) high and 7" (18cm) wide from the fall-colored fabrics. Cut the leftover scraps into strips approx. ¾" (2cm) wide and set aside for the trunks and branches. Make up the strips for the branches and trunks with other pieces of light and dark fabric if you need to, as the scraps may not be enough. It might also be handy to have a few trees in reserve when you are assembling the quilt.

Place a rectangle of fabric vertically on the cutting mat and remove all 4 corners, cutting at an angle of 45° to make the triangles as large as possible. You can use a triangular ruler to make this cut, if you wish. Pin the triangular corners together and set aside. Divide the tree piece lengthways down the center (this is where the trunk will be inserted).

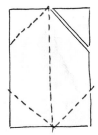

Cut out rectangles of approx. 10" x 7" (25 x 18cm), trim off all 4 corners at an angle of 45° (using a triangular ruler if required). Cut vertically down the center.

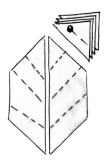

Set the 4 triangles aside and make cuts for the branches.

Make three to four cuts running upward at an angle from the center line of the piece—these will be the branches. Insert the strips you made for the branches in a contrasting color and then insert the vertical trunk, as described in Lesson 7. Reattach the 2 top triangles that were set aside.

Slide all the pieces apart before inserting the short branches first.

Insert a trunk between the 2 halves and reattach the 2 top triangles.

Pin the 2 remaining triangles to the tree block.

Pin the the remaining 2 triangles to the tree block so that you can easily find them when you are matching up colors later. Use dark branches with light tree fabrics and light branches with dark tree fabrics. Make approx. 230 tree blocks in this way, but don't trim anything to size yet.

Sewing plan

To assemble the quilt you will need a pin board of sufficient size or a large surface where you can lay out the blocks. Starting with the top row, place a row of 16 tree blocks side by side. Arrange a second row of 17 trees, offset so that the trunks of the bottom row of trees align with the edges of the tree blocks in the row above. Lay out 13 horizontal rows. Sort the trees into color groups and spread out any individually striking trees across the quilt; you can refer to the photo or make your own arrangement.

1st row, top edge: cut 16 light turquoise squares of approx. 4" x 4" (10 x 10cm) for the sky and divide each square in half diagonally. Take the 2 tree triangles pinned to the first block and join a turquoise triangle to each one along their long edges. Join the 2 squares together with the tree triangles facing each other; press the seam allowance. Join the piece to the top edge of the tree block so that the top edge of the square represents the sky. Repeat across the entire row.

1st to 12th rows, bottom edges: Working block by block with the triangles pinned to the tree blocks, join a triangle from one of the adjacent trees in the row below to the bottom corners of each tree block. Join a triangle from the tree below left to the

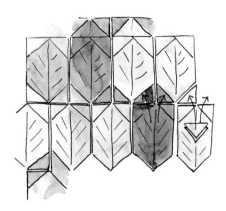

Arrange the tree blocks in 13 offset rows of 16 and 17 trees respectively. Working with the triangles pinned to the tree blocks, join one of the triangles to the bottom right-hand corner of the tree block that is above it and to the left, and join the other triangle to the bottom left-hand corner of the tree block above it and to the right.

Top row: working with the triangles pinned to the tree blocks, join the tree triangles to the sky triangles along their long edges. Join the 2 squares with the tree triangles facing each other: join these double blocks to the top edge of the tree block of the matching color.

Trim each block to exactly the same size and place it back into the layout. Join all the blocks together and neaten the side edges.

left-hand corner, and a triangle from the tree below right to the right-hand corner. Press each block as you work.

Trim all the tree blocks to the same size: in our 1st row, they were 6" (15cm) wide and 10¾" (27cm) high and in all the other rows they were 6" (15cm) wide and 8" (20cm) high. The trees in every second row (the rows with 17 trees) will overhang to the left- and right-hand sides.

13th row, bottom edge: cut 16 dark turquoise squares of approx. 4" x 4" (10 x 10cm) for the earth and divide each square in half diagonally. Join these triangles to the bottom corners of the trees in the bottom row. Press and trim the blocks as above.

Assembly
(Lesson 10)
First, join the tree blocks to make horizontal rows and then join these together. Trim off the excess half trees at the side edges.

Making up the quilt and quilting
(Lessons 12 and 13)
Lay the backing, batting, and pressed front panel one on top of the other. Quilt arched treetops across the blocks, either as simple lines or as sweeping ornamental lines in the upper treetops. Quilt vertical lines reaching right to the edge onto the triangles at the top and bottom edges. Trim the quilt edges straight again.

Binding
(Lesson 14)
Bind the basted quilt edge with wine-red bias tape.

Quilting suggestion: decorate the treetops with ornamental patterns.

Meandering River
55" x 27½" (140 x 70cm)

The twists and turns of the river give this design life. The river banks are edged with red piping and the blue of the water gets lighter as the river wanders away into the distance.

■ Materials
Fabrics
- 8" (20cm) each of at least 20 different fabrics in shades of light blue to deep turquoise, or lots of strips 1¼"–2" (3–5cm) wide for the river
- 1¾ yd. (1.50m) dark brown fabric for the land
- 1¾ yd. (1.50m) plain red fabric for the piping

Other materials
- 59" x 36" (150 x 90cm) backing fabric
- 59" x 36" (150 x 90cm) batting
- quilting thread in brown
- water-soluble marker pen

■ Method
Making the river
Arrange the blue fabrics by shade from light to dark. Cut strips 1¼"–2" (3–5cm) wide from selvage to selvage. Cut the strips freehand without the aid of a ruler, so the water looks natural.

Make a large strip section 59" (150cm) long (the approximate length of the quilt), as described in Lesson 5. The light fabrics should be at the top and the dark fabrics at the bottom. First, join the strips along their long edges with a curved seam (Lesson 6) to make sections of approx. 8" (20cm) deep, then join a slightly wider strip to the top and bottom edge of each section.

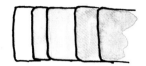

Sort the water fabrics by shade.

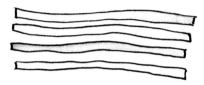

Cut lots of freehand strips.

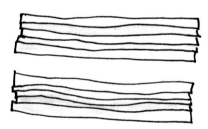

Join the strips along their long edges to make sections approx. 8" (20cm) deep, retaining the color sequence from light (at the top) to dark (at the bottom).

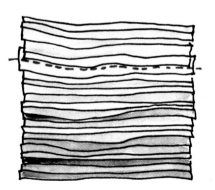

Join up as many sections with curved seams as you need to make the full length of the quilt.

Press the sections and join them together using a curved seam. Press the finished piece well and neaten—you might need to press any bumps flat and tidy up some of the seams.

Making the riverbanks using piping techniques
(Lesson 8)
Spread the red piping fabric out over the brown landscape fabric, right sides facing. Draw the meandering line of the river. Start at the bottom with a wide riverbed and make it narrower as it goes up the quilt. Draw freehand or refer to our quilt for the shape. You might like to make an enlarged template and trace the outline.

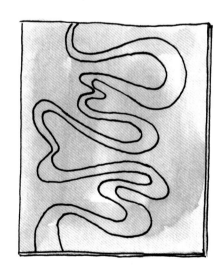

Place the red piping fabric on top of the brown fabric, right sides facing, and draw the shape of the river. Sew along both the lines.

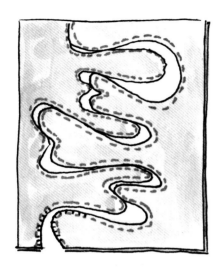

Cut out the fabric between the lines, leaving a seam allowance.

Clip the seam allowances and push the piping fabric over the edge to the wrong side. Flatten the edges and baste.

Sew a line of short stitches along the riverbank line you have drawn. Cut both fabrics along the line on the "water side," leaving a seam allowance. You will now have 2 halves that you can work on individually. Clip the seam allowances and fold the red piping fabric over the edge to the wrong side. Don't let the sight of such a weird shape worry you; carefully flatten the seam edges and, where possible, let the red piping fabric stick out approx. 1/16" (1–2mm). Baste along the edge of the workpiece to hold the piping in place.

Press both sections of riverbank and arrange them, brown sides uppermost, on the top of the water-strip section.

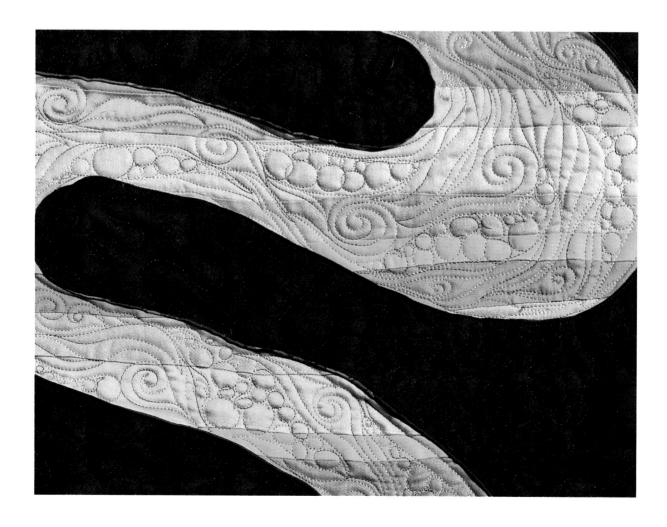

Pin the edges carefully and make a line of long basting stitches ½" (1cm) in from the riverbank. Stitch along the edges of the riverbanks with brown thread. Remove the basting thread and trim off the excess water and piping fabrics on the back, leaving a seam allowance.

Making up the quilt and quilting
(Lessons 12 and 13)
Lay the backing, batting, and pressed front panel one on top of the other. Quilt flowing water lines, whirlpools, and eddies onto the river and alternate bands of densely packed and spread-out patterning across the land sections. Quilt right up to the riverbanks. Trim the edges straight.

Binding
(Lesson 14)
Bind the basted edges of the quilt with dark brown bias tape.

Finishing
Make a hanger casing and sew to the top edge at the back.

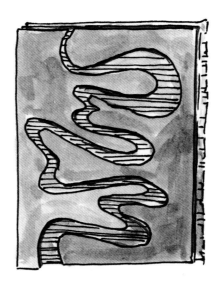

Pin both sections of riverbank to the water section you have made.

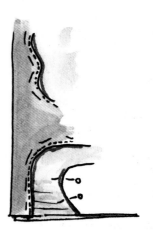

Pin the river banks and baste in place before stitching along the edges. Trim off the excess piping and water fabrics on the back, leaving a seam allowance along the riverbank.

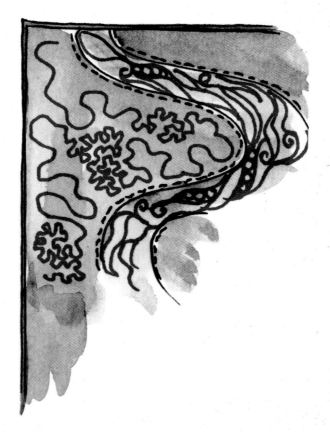

Quilting suggestion.

Lesson 10

FINISHING

Lesson 10:
Assembling Blocks of Equal Size

Arrange the blocks of your quilt on a work surface or the floor until you are happy with the design.

Number the vertical rows in your head as 1, 2, 3, and so on. Mark the top blocks with a pin.

With right sides facing, place the blocks of row 2 on top of the blocks of row 1.

Make a staggered pile of the pairs of blocks, starting with the bottom pair so the top pair is at the top of the pile. Place the pile to the left of your sewing machine (a short distance between your workstation and the sewing machine means you won't get the blocks the wrong way round!).

Starting with the top pair of blocks, sew a seam exactly ¼" (0.5cm) along the right-hand edges of the pairs of blocks. Do NOT cut the threads between the blocks. Now join up the horizontal seams of the chain of blocks, starting with both the bottom pairs. Lay the first pair onto the next, right sides facing, and join the edges with a ¼" (0.5cm) seam. Where the seams meet, fold one of the seam allowances upward and the other one downward.

Carry on like this, making sure that the part of the double row you have sewn is always at the top and the next pair to be sewn is at the bottom. This will allow you to keep an eye on the seam allowances and know in which direction the next seam allowance has to be folded.

Finish the double row and press all the seam allowances of the horizontal seam downward. The pin you put in at the beginning will help you to find which way is "up" for the row.

Make more double rows of blocks from vertical rows 3 and 4, 5 and 6, and so on.

Press the seam allowances of all the horizontal seams of the second double row upward, press those of the third row downward, and so on.

If your quilt has an odd number of rows, assemble the last 3 rows as follows: join up the long seams of the penultimate 2 rows as described, but before you close up the horizontal seams, join the blocks of the last row. Don't cut the threads between the blocks. The horizontal seams will be 3 blocks wide in this case.

Once all the double rows are assembled, join them up. The pressed seam allowances should now all be lying in alternate directions and you will have nice flat seams. Finally, press the front of the quilt, first from the wrong side and then from the right side.

Advantages
Laying out the blocks in systematic, staggered piles means that you can arrange the front of the quilt in a different room from where you keep your sewing machine. Transport the piles of blocks on your long quilting ruler as if you were carrying them on a tray.

Sorting and arranging systematic piles reduces the risk of getting the blocks the wrong way round to a minimum.

Stitching the blocks together in chains, where the threads between the blocks are not cut off, prevents the blocks from being inserted the wrong way round.

If you place the piles of blocks to the left of your sewing machine, you will have the shortest distance from workstation to needle—this will also help you get the blocks the right way round.

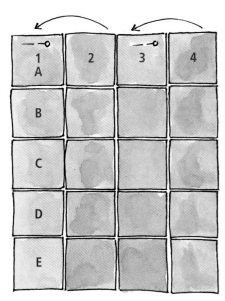

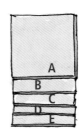

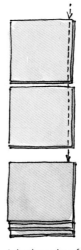

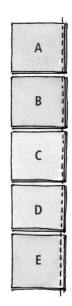

Place the blocks of vertical row 2 on top of the blocks of vertical row 1, right sides facing. Repeat with the subsequent rows.

Collect up the pairs of blocks and make a pile, starting with the bottom pair (so the top pair is at the top).

Join the pairs of blocks along the right-hand edges.

Do NOT cut the threads between the pairs.

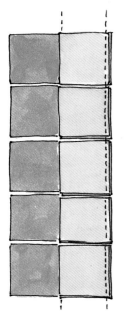

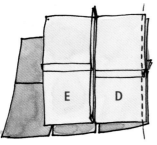

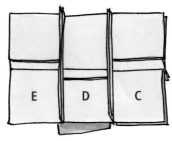

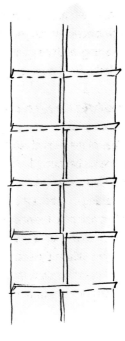

The solution to the last three of an odd number of horizontal rows.

Join the pairs with horizontal seams, starting with the bottom pair of blocks.

The pairs you have joined will always be at the top. Fold down the seam allowances in alternating directions.

Press all the horizontal seams of the first double row downward, press the next double row upward, the next downward, and so on.

Lesson 11:
Adding a Border

Measuring the quilt

Always measure your quilt horizontally and vertically through the center of the finished, pressed quilt front panel, never along the border. The length of the border strips should be determined by these dimensions. Just to be sure, measure the quilt front again after sewing on each border strip.

Adding a border with straight corners

Neaten the edges of the quilt or pillow front if necessary. Work out a suitable width for the strip and cut out the border strips. Join several strips to make the length required.

First, join the border strips to the 2 long sides of the quilt; the strips for the top and bottom edges are sewn on last. The length of the strips for the top and bottom edges are taken from the width of the quilt plus the width of the 2 side border strips. To find this measurement, measure the quilt again across the center.

Adding a border with corner sections

Corner sections are generally square and always the same width as the border. Cut the border strips to the same length as the edges of the quilt. Join a corner section to each end of the top and bottom border strips, pressing the seam allowances

toward the border side. Join the border strips to the long sides of the quilt first and press the seam allowances outward. Now join the 2 border strips with their attached corner sections to the top and bottom edges of the quilt.

Adding a border with mitered corners

Neaten the edges of the quilt or pillow front if necessary. Work out a suitable width for the strip and cut out the border strips. Join several strips to make the length required. You can work out the length in the following way: length of the quilt edge, plus twice the width of the border strips, plus twice the seam allowances, plus approx. 2" (5cm) for good luck.

Join the border strips to the 4 edges of the quilt panel. Pin the strips from the center so that there is the same amount of excess fabric at each end. Begin and end the seam at the corner. Don't sew over the seam allowances. Press the seam allowances outward.

With right sides facing, fold the front of the quilt in half diagonally and, using a ruler, extend the diagonal line of the fold across the border strip. Stitch the border along this line. Trim off the excess fabric at the corner.

Press the seam allowances flat. Make all 4 corners of the quilt in the same manner.

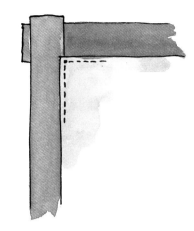

Mitered corner: sew right up to the corner.

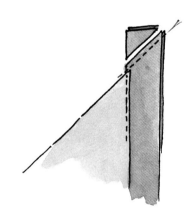

Fold the quilt diagonally. Extend the line of the fold across the border strip. Join the seams in the border strip. Trim off the excess fabric at the corner.

Piping

Piping is a folded strip of fabric that is sewn into a seam; only a fraction of an inch of the piping may be visible. The piping fabric should always be in a contrasting color. It can be sewn into the seams of binding strips, between the quilt center panel and the border strip, or between 2 different colored border strips.

Cut a piping strip exactly ¾" (2cm) wide and of sufficient length, and fold it in half lengthways, with wrong sides facing. Press it, and with the raw fabric edges facing outward, attach the strip to the edge of the quilt front, joining it on with a ⅛" (3mm) seam. Align the border fabric strip edge to edge, right sides facing, and pin in place. Sew a ¼" (0.5cm) seam along the edge through all the layers of fabric. When you unfold the border fabric, just under ⅛" (3mm) of the piping will be visible.

Cut out the piping and fold it lengthways, wrong sides facing.

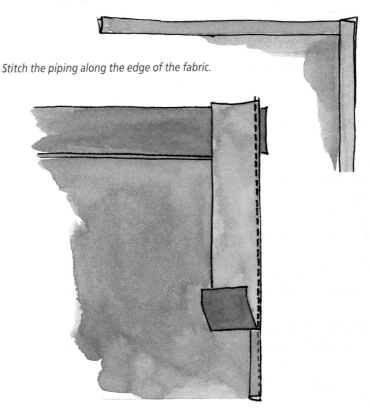

Stitch the piping along the edge of the fabric.

Stitch the piping into the next seam you make.

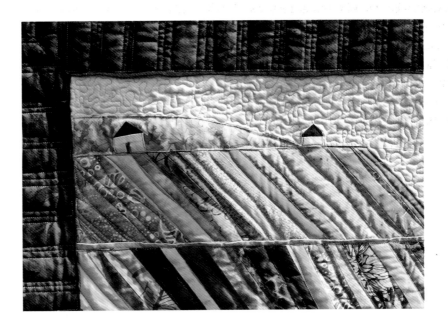

Lesson 12:
Assembling the Quilt Layers

Carefully press the finished front panel of the quilt. Cut a piece of quilt backing fabric that is about 4" (10cm) larger on all sides than the quilt front. Cut the batting to the same size as the backing fabric.

Tip
If you have to connect sections of batting, join the edges with large overlock stitches. Use normal sewing thread (it won't shrink when it's washed) and don't pull the stitches too tight, to avoid making any bumps.

Spread out the backing, right side downward, on a large work surface and stick down the corners with tape. Place the batting on top and smooth it out flat.

Lay the quilt front panel on top, right side up and smooth it out flat, starting from the center and working toward the edges.

Baste diagonally across the front of the quilt at intervals of about a handbreadth. Push the basting needle right through to the work surface and push the tip back through to the front without placing your hand underneath the quilt. This will help to avoid wrinkles and the layers won't get out of position. Work from as close to the center of the quilt as possible to the outside or start along one outer edge. Continue to

the opposite edge, row after row of basting stitches; this will allow you to push any wrinkles that might occur toward the raw fabric edge.

Trim the excess backing fabric and the batting to within approx. 2" (5cm) from the edge of front panel of the quilt. Now quilt the design by hand or with your sewing machine.

Tip
You can secure the layers for small quilts and pillows using a practical, low-tack spray glue. The sticky substance evaporates on its own after a while, but will hold long enough for you to finish machine quilting.

Lesson 13:
Quilting with a Sewing Machine

Straight line quilting
Use the feed dogs of your sewing machine (the teeth under the needle). If possible attach an even-feed presser foot to your machine; this will help to prevent the fabrics puckering. Sew along predrawn straight lines (for example, when grid quilting) or into the seams (used for border strips). Use the same color top and bobbin thread, in case the bobbin thread shows through to the front.

Outline quilting
In outline quilting, the quilt line goes around a particular pattern, either in the seam or at a distance of a seam allowance all round the pattern. Here you are machine quilting without drawing lines first.

Grid quilting
A regular grid of straight lines is drawn up and down and/or diagonally across the quilt. Here you are machine quilting along predrawn lines.

Freehand machine quilting
Attach the darning or free-motion foot of the sewing machine (very rarely, you will be able to quilt freehand without using the presser foot at all). Lower the feed dogs and/or set the tension of the needle bar to 0 if possible. Use the same color top and bobbin thread and loosen the top thread tension a little if possible. Select straight stitch; it doesn't matter which stitch length you go for. The 3 layers of the quilt should be basted one on top of the other, or stuck with low-tack spray glue. Try out the technique on a practice piece first.

Lower the presser foot (this is important for the thread tension). With some types of machine, the presser foot should be lowered only halfway. Apply even pressure to the foot pedal and, using both hands, guide the area to be quilted through the sewing machine. Place your hands flat on the quilt to the right and left of the needle and sew at a relatively brisk pace.

As a first exercise, try to quilt wavy lines that you can gradually extend into meandering lines to make the so-called "stippling" effect. With a little practice, the stitches will be all the same length and your quilting lines will be regular. Oversew the threads at the beginning and end of the quilting line with a few stitches or take the thread to the wrong side of the quilt and tie it off.

Stippling and other fill patterns

To quilt a stippled pattern, you need to quilt closely-spaced meandering lines that do not

Tip

Textured rubber gardening gloves or latex gloves are extremely useful when trying to guide the quilt at a consistent speed through the machine.

overlap across the quilt. You can make up different patterns: series of loops, whorls, flame shapes, circles, blades of grass, triangles, squares, teardrops, spirals, arches, tendrils, flowers, or leaves. Stitch in a continuous line and try to interrupt your work as little as possible.

Quilting motifs

Draw out a quilting motif with lines as continuous as possible, and the least number of breaks. Quilt along the lines. With a bit of practice you will be able to quilt beautiful motifs without even drawing a pattern first.

Text

Practice writing letters and words in cursive script. Sew the cross-bars of the t's at the same time as you quilt the uprights and dot the i's straight away, or just leave the dots out. If you forget the dots at the time, you can go back and add them later, and don't worry about quilting small connecting lines between the parts of the letters. Words are connected with gently curving lines. Don't predraw the designs. When you can write your name with your sewing machine, you can sign your quilt.

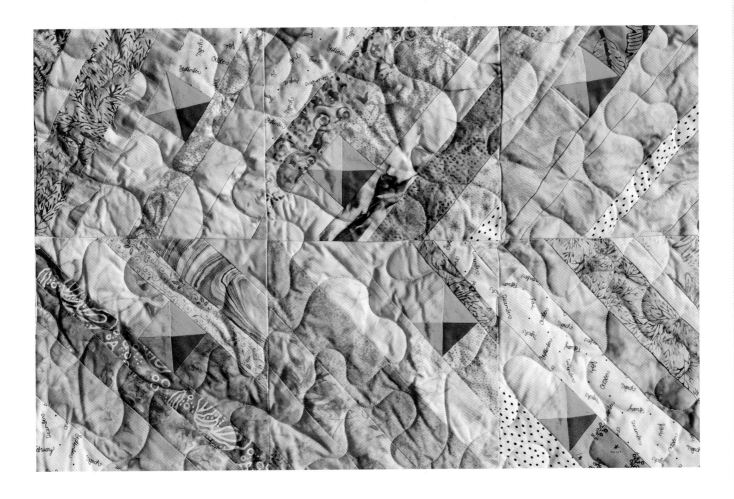

Lesson 14:
Binding a Quilt

The binding is the outermost strip of fabric that encloses the edge of the quilt. It is not attached until all the quilting has been completed.

Preparing the quilt

To neaten the edges of the quilt, draw a line using a straight edge and a water-soluble marker along all the edges of the quilt—you could use a long ruler here. To make the corners exactly 90°, place an object of a reasonable size with a right-angled corner on the quilt (e.g. a piece of cardboard, a picture frame, etc.), or use the corner of your work table; the grid on your cutting mat is perfect for smaller projects. Baste around the edges of the quilt, along the lines you have drawn, then trim off all the excess fabric and the batting 1⁄16" (1–2mm) outside this line. The quilt is now ready for binding.

Tip
A piece of aluminum flat or straight edge from the DIY store makes an excellent long ruler.

Straight-cut, folded binding

For straight binding, cut the strip of fabric to a width of 2½" (6cm), unless another measurement is given. Join as many strips as you need to make up the length of the total perimeter of the quilt.

Fold the binding strip in half lengthways, with wrong sides facing, and press. Place the strip along the edge of the quilt with the raw edges facing outward and make a ¼" (0.5cm) seam along its length.

Trim off the excess fabric at the end of the first quilt edge. Fold the closed edge of the strip back to the wrong side of the quilt and pin it securely in place. Now join the next strip to the adjacent edge, leaving approx. ¾" (2cm) overlap at the beginning, so you can fold a nice clean corner. Attach the first 3 strips in this manner. When sewing on the fourth strip, leave an additional ¾" (2cm) excess fabric at the bottom corner. Carefully fold the strips back to the wrong side of the quilt all around, pin, and hem by hand exactly along the seam line.

Make the corners by folding the raw, overlapping, short edge of the strip down toward the quilt edge and then folding the strip back to the wrong side of the quilt. Hand sew the short edge of the binding at the corner.

Sew on a straight-cut strip of fabric folded lengthways.

Fold the strip over to the wrong side and pin in place.

Leave a little excess fabric when you attach the next strip.

Make a straight corner and sew up the folded edge by hand on the wrong side of the quilt.

Lesson 14

Binding with ready-made bias tape

Buy ready-folded bias tape in a suitable color (or use a bias tape-maker to make some yourself from your own fabric). Make sure that it is long enough to go all the way round the quilt plus an extra 8" (20cm) or so for good measure. Place the bias tape right side down along the quilt edge and open out the right-hand edge. Sew the strip to the quilt edge along the pressed fold. Leave ¾" (2cm) excess fabric at the beginning of the next strip and at the end of the last strip, as previously described. Fold the bias tape back to the wrong side of the quilt and hem it by hand along the folded edge directly along the seam. Make straight corners.

Changing the color of your binding strip

Finish off the seam of the binding strip of the first color at exactly the point where the color is to change and trim off the strip ½" (1cm) farther along. Fold up this excess fabric and place the strip in the next color on top, with the beginning of the new strip overlapping the first one by approx. ½" (1cm). Join on the new strip.

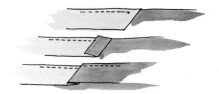

Changing the color of a binding strip.

Open out the right-hand edge of the bias tape and sew it to the edge of the quilt along the fold.

Fold the bias tape over to the wrong side and hem by hand.

Lesson 15:
Inserting a Zipper in a Pillow Cover

Cut the pillow backing fabric to the same width as the pillow front but 4" (10cm) longer.

Lay the backing fabric lengthways onto the cutting mat. Make a horizontal cut to remove the bottom third of the fabric. With right sides facing, place the cut edges together and mark the beginning and end of the zipper with a pin.

Sew a seam 2" (5cm) in from the edge, in this manner:

1. From the top edge to the top zipper marker, use normal-length stitches;
2. Use a few backstitches at the top marker point;
3. From the top marker down to the bottom marker, use your longest stitches (basting stitches);
4. Use a few backstitches at the bottom marker point;
5. And from the bottom marker down to the bottom edge, use normal-length stitches.

Remove marker pins. Unfold and press the seam. Fold under both edges of the seam allowance to the stitching and press again.

Alternatively, you could neaten the edges using zigzag stitches.

Unpick the seam at the beginning of the basting stitches to make an opening approx. 2" (5cm) wide. Place the zipper on the wrong side of the fabric along the basted seam, right side facing the seam. Push the slider of the zipper to the front through the opening in the seam. Pin the zipper in place with extra long pins.

Working from the front of the fabric, sew a seam ¼" (0.5cm) from the right-hand edge of the seam, in this manner:

1. Start at the arrow.
2. Open the zipper 2" (5cm).
3. Sew as far as the slider of the zipper.
4. Lift the presser foot and close the zipper.
5. Carry on sewing to the end of the zipper.
6. Sew a seam across the end of the zipper (either tapering to a point or straight across).
7. Turn the pillow backing by 180°.
8. Sew along the other side of the zipper as far as the slider.
9. Lift the presser foot and open the zipper 2" (5cm).
10. Sew to the end.
11. Sew another end seam at the top end.

Remove the pins and unpick the remaining basting stitches using a seam ripper. Pick out the last little bits of thread from the edges of the fabric.

Finishing the pillow

When hand quilting a pillow front, make sure you quilt inside the central area of 20" x 20" (50 x 50cm) so that the quilting threads won't be snipped off when you cut the front to size. Trim the finshed and quilted pillow front to exactly 20½" x 20½" (52 x 52cm).

If you have quilted the pillow front by machine, cut it to 20½" x 20½" (52 x 52cm)—it won't matter if you cut through the quilting lines as the edges will be incorporated into the seams of the pillow.

Open the zipper by about 4" (10cm). Place the pillow backing with its zipper right side up on your worktop and lay the 20½" x 20½" (52 x 52cm) pillow front right side down on top of it. Make sure that the motif on the front of the pillow is the right way up.

With right sides facing, pin the pillow front and back together and sew a ¼" (0.5cm) seam around the pillow. Trim the excess fabric at the edges of the pillow backing. Neaten all the edges with zigzag stitches.

Turn the pillow right side out through the zipper opening and fill it with a pillow form.

Tip

The following technique will ensure beautifully shaped corners: push your index finger into the pillow right up to the corner. With the other hand, first fold the seam allowances of the corner in horizontally, then push the neighboring seam down vertically over it. Press on it with your thumb and hold the corner tightly between your thumb and forefinger. Turn the corner right side out without loosening your grip. Once turned right side out, the corner will hold its shape and you will not have to trim the seam allowances.

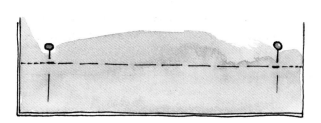

Prepare the seam for the zipper. Sew long basting stitches between the pin marker points.

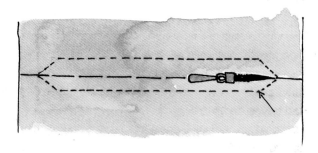

Sewing in a zipper (arrow = starting point). You may need to open or close the zipper as you sew the seam.

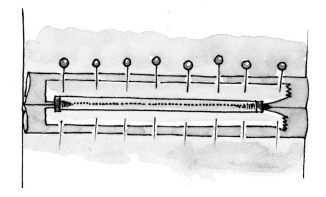

Pin the zipper securely in place from the wrong side using long pins. Push the slider of the zipper through the opened part of the seam.

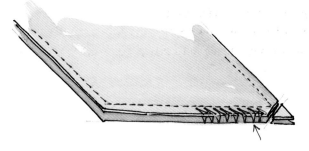

Lay the pillow sections one on top of the other and stitch around the edge. Trim the edge of the pillow backing and clip off the corners (or see tip box). Neaten the edges with zigzag stitches.

Lesson 15

NOTE: Page numbers in *italics* indicate projects.